THIRD EDITION
SUMMIT 2B

ENGLISH FOR TODAY'S WORLD
with WORKBOOK

JOAN SASLOW
ALLEN ASCHER

Summit: English for Today's World   Level 2B with Workbook, Third Edition

Pearson, 221 River Street, Hoboken, NJ 07030

Staff credits: The people who made up the *Summit* team representing editorial, production, design, manufacturing, and marketing are Pietro Alongi, Rhea Banker, Peter Benson, Stephanie Bullard, Jennifer Castro, Tracey Munz Cataldo, Rosa Chapinal, Aerin Csigay, Dave Dickey, Gina DiLillo, Christopher Leonowicz, Laurie Neaman, Alison Pei, Sherri Pemberton, Jennifer Raspiller, Mary Rich, Courtney Steers, Katherine Sullivan, and Paula Van Ells.

Cover credit: Tonis Pan/Shutterstock

Text composition: emc design ltd

Library of Congress Cataloging-in-Publication Data

Names: Saslow, Joan M., author. | Ascher, Allen, author.
Title: Summit : English for today's world / Joan Saslow and Allen Ascher.
Description: Third Edition. | White Plains, NY : Pearson Education, [2017]
Identifiers: LCCN 2016017942| ISBN 9780134096070 (book w/ CD) | ISBN
  9780134176888 (book w/ CD) | ISBN 013409607X (book w/ CD)
Subjects: LCSH: English language--Textbooks for foreign speakers. | English
  language--Rhetoric. | English language--Sound recording for foreign
  speakers.
Classification: LCC PE1128 .S2757 2017 | DDC 428.2/4--dc23
LC record available at https://lccn.loc.gov/2016017942

Student Book

Photo credits: Original photography Mike Cohen. Page 64 (tl) Kurhan/Fotolia, (tr) Hill Creek Pictures/UpperCut Images/Getty Images, (br) Birkholz/E+/Getty Images , (bl) EMPPhotography/E+/Getty Images; p. 66 Daisy Daisy/Fotolia; p. 68 Tetra Images/Getty Images; p. 69 nakophotography/Fotolia; p. 70 (t) Thinkstock Images/Stockbyte/Getty Images, (m) Petert2/Fotolia, (b) Digital Vision/Photodisc/Getty Images; p. 71 Robin Nelson/ZUMA Press/Newscom; p. 73 Photographyttl/Fotolia; p. 74 (A) Cosid/Shutterstock, (B) Juriah Mosin/Shutterstock, (C) Til Vogt/Shutterstock, (D) Pathdoc/Fotolia, (E) Objowl/Shutterstock; p. 75 Dave/Les Jacobs/Blend Images/Getty Images; p. 77 (t) kupicoo/E+/Getty Images, (m) kupicoo/E+/Getty Images, (b) Monkey Business Images/Shutterstock (diamond) Atiketta Sangasaeng/Shutterstock; p. 80 (l) kubais/Shutterstock, (r) Steven Heap/123RF; p. 84 t_fuji/Fotolia; p. 86 SWP/Fotolia; p. 87 Digitalskillet/E+/Getty Images; p. 88 BillionPhotos.com/Fotolia, Rick Gomez/Blend Images/Getty Images, Huntstock/Getty Images, Scott Griessel/Fotolia, BillionPhotos.com/Fotolia, Istockalypse Elkor/Getty Images, Bst2012/Fotolia, Monkey Business/Fotolia; p. 89 StockLite/Shutterstock; p. 90 VLADGRIN/Shutterstock; p. 91 Nomad_Soul/Fotolia; p. 92 DragonImages/Fotolia; p. 93 Indeed/Getty Images, JackF/Fotolia, Minerva Studio/Fotolia, Felix Mizioznikov/Shutterstock, Jeanette Dietl/Shutterstock, leungchopan/Fotolia; p. 94 (Einstein) akg images/Newscom, (Ramanujan) Nick Higham/Alamy Stock Photo; p. 98 Anibal/Fotolia; p. 99 Michal Krakowiak/Getty Images; p. 100 (Olsen) Carol Francavilla/AP Images, (Jobs) Terry Schmitt/UPI/Newscom, (Gates) Richard Ellis/Alamy Stock Photo; p. 101 (tl) Jun Dangoy/Fotolia, (tr) Patrick/Fotolia, (br) VictorHabbickVisions/Science Photo Library/Getty Images, (bl) Hxdyl/Fotolia; p. 102 (headset) wayne_0216/Fotolia, (finger) Mihaperosa/Fotolia, (atom) Petecek/Fotolia; p. 103 Serge Black/Fotolia; p. 104 (redwoods) Tomasz Zajda/Fotolia, (Milarch) Dusty Christensen/MCT/Newscom, (Tuy) Jeremy_Holden/Photoshot/Newscom; p. 105 Design56/Fotolia, Robraine/Shutterstock; p. 106 Epicurean/Vetta/Getty Images; p. 107 (wedding) Paylessimages/Fotolia, (babies) Blaine Harrington III/Alamy Stock Photo, (wheelchair) Kzenon/Shutterstock; p. 110 (t) Bst2012/Fotolia, (b) XiXinXing/Shutterstock; p. 111 (park backdrop) Trofotodesign/Fotolia; p. 113 Djoronimo/Fotolia; p. 114 (t) StockLite/Fotolia, (m) Daniel Ingold/Getty Images, (b) LDprod/Shutterstock; p. 115 (l) James Brunker/Alamy Stock Photo, (c) Natalie Behring/Newscom, (tr) Peter Muller/Cultura/Getty Images, (b) Dean Bertoncelj/Shutterstock; p. 117 Federico Rostangno/Fotolia; p. 118 (l) Dmitrimaruta/Fotolia, (r) Alen-D/Fotolia.

Illustration credits: Aptara pp. 67, 78; el Primo Ramon pp. 62, 82, 119.

Workbook

Photo credits: Page 63: Ivan Cholakov/Shutterstock; 65: Monkey Business/Fotolia; 68: Fotolia; 70 (center): Yayoicho/Fotolia; 70 (top): Carlos Santa Maria/Fotolia; 74 (bottom, center): Everett Historical/Shutterstock; 74 (bottom, left): Ksenia Ragozina/Shutterstock; 74 (bottom, right): Dora Zett/Shutterstock; 74 (top, center): Fat Jackey/Shutterstock; 74 (top, left): Livefocus/Shutterstock; 74 (top, right): Cranach/Shutterstock; 77: Tupungato/Fotolia; 79: Nejron Photo/Shutterstock; 82: David Stuart Productions/Shutterstock; 86: Artbalance/Fotolia; 87 (bottom): Kkolosov/Fotolia; 87 (bottom, center): Burlingham/Fotolia; 87 (top): Nicholas Piccillo/Fotolia; 87 (top, center): Pathdoc/Fotolia; 92: Georgios Kollidas/Shutterstock; 93: Pjmorley/Shutterstock; 95: DragonImages/Fotolia; 96 (bottom): Kurhan/Fotolia; 96 (bottom, center): Minerva Studio/Fotolia; 96 (top): Uber Images/Fotolia; 96 (top, center): Sakkmesterke/Fotolia; 097: DPA/SOA/The Image Works; 099: Everett Collection; 102 (bottom): Odua Images/Shutterstock; 102 (top): Daseaford/Fotolia; 103: Everett Collection Historical/Alamy Stock Photo; 108: J. Lekavicius/Shutterstock; 110: Mumindurmaz35/Fotolia; 114 (bottom): Drobot Dean/Fotolia; 114 (bottom, center): Amble Design/Shutterstock; 114 (top): Egyptian Studio/Fotolia; 114 (top, center): Hurricanehank/Shutterstock; 115: Mary Evans Picture Library/Alamy Stock Photo; 117: Dailin/Shutterstock; 118: William STEVENS/Alamy Stock Photo; 119: Blend Images/Alamy Stock Photo; 121: William87/Fotolia.

Illustration Credits: Leanne Franson: pages 65, 101; ElectraGraphics, Inc.: pages 101, 102.

Printed in the United States of America

ISBN-10: 0-13-449890-9
ISBN-13: 978-0-13-449890-4
1 17

Contents

LEARNING OBJECTIVES

UNIT	COMMUNICATION GOALS	VOCABULARY	GRAMMAR
UNIT 1 **Dreams and Goals** PAGE 2	• Ask about someone's background • Discuss career and study plans • Compare your dreams and goals in life • Describe job qualifications	• Job applications • Collocations for career and study plans • Describing dreams and goals **Word Study:** • Collocations with <u>have</u> and <u>get</u> for qualifications	• Simultaneous and sequential past actions: review and expansion • Completed and uncompleted past actions closely related to the present **GRAMMAR BOOSTER** • Describing past actions and events: review • Stative verbs: non-action and action meanings
UNIT 2 **Character and Responsibility** PAGE 14	• Describe the consequences of lying • Express regret and take responsibility • Explore where values come from • Discuss how best to help others	• Taking or avoiding responsibility • Philanthropic work	• Adjective clauses: review and expansion • "Comment" clauses **GRAMMAR BOOSTER** • Adjective clauses: overview • Grammar for Writing: adjective clauses with quantifiers • Grammar for Writing: reduced adjective clauses
UNIT 3 **Fears, Hardships, and Heroism** PAGE 26	• Express frustration, empathy, and encouragement • Describe how fear affects you physically • Discuss overcoming handicaps and hardships • Examine the nature of heroism	• Expressing frustration, empathy, and encouragement • Physical effects of fear **Word Study:** • Using parts of speech	• Clauses with <u>no matter</u> • Using <u>so</u> … (<u>that</u>) or <u>such</u> … (<u>that</u>) to explain results **GRAMMAR BOOSTER** • Embedded questions: review and common errors • Non-count nouns made countable • Nouns used in both countable and uncountable sense
UNIT 4 **Getting Along with Others** PAGE 38	• Discuss how to overcome shortcomings • Acknowledge inconsiderate behavior • Explain how you handle anger • Explore the qualities of friendship	• Shortcomings • Expressing and controlling anger	• Adverb clauses of condition • Cleft sentences: review and expansion **GRAMMAR BOOSTER** • Grammar for Writing: more conjunctions and transitions • Cleft sentences: more on meaning and use
UNIT 5 **Humor** PAGE 50	• Discuss the health benefits of laughter • Respond to something funny • Analyze what makes us laugh • Explore the limits of humor	• Ways to respond to jokes and other funny things • Common types of jokes • Practical jokes	• Indirect speech: backshifts in tense and time expressions • Questions in indirect speech **GRAMMAR BOOSTER** • Imperatives in indirect speech • Changes to pronouns and possessives • <u>Say</u>, <u>tell</u>, and <u>ask</u> • Other reporting verbs

CONVERSATION STRATEGIES	LISTENING / PRONUNCIATION	READING	WRITING
• Use <u>Thanks for asking</u> to express appreciation for someone's interest. • Use <u>Correct me if I'm wrong</u>, but … to tentatively assert what you believe about someone or something. • Say <u>I've given it some thought and …</u> to introduce a thoughtful opinion. • Informally ask for directions by saying <u>Steer me in the right direction</u>. • Say <u>As a matter of fact</u> to present a relevant fact. • Offer assistance with <u>I'd be more than happy to</u>. • Say <u>I really appreciate it</u> to express gratitude.	**Listening Skills:** • Listen to activate vocabulary • Listen for main ideas • Listen to confirm content • Listen for supporting details • Listen to infer **PRONUNCIATION BOOSTER** • Sentence stress and intonation: review	**Texts:** • An application for employment • An article about two famous people • An article about good and bad interview behavior • A job advertisement • A résumé **Skills / strategies:** • Understand idioms and expressions • Confirm information • Apply ideas	**Task:** • Write a traditional cover letter to an employer **Skill:** • A formal cover letter
• Admit having made a mistake by apologizing with <u>I'm really sorry</u>, but … • Confirm that someone agrees to an offer with <u>if that's OK</u>. • Use <u>That's really not necessary</u> to politely turn down an offer. • Take responsibility for a mistake by saying <u>Please accept my apology</u>.	**Listening Skills:** • Listen to infer information • Listen to support an opinion • Listen for main ideas • Listen to classify • Listen to confirm content • Listen for point of view • Listen to summarize • Listen to draw conclusions **PRONUNCIATION BOOSTER** • Emphatic stress and pitch to express emotion	**Texts:** • A survey about taking or avoiding responsibility • An article about lying • A textbook article about the development of values • Dictionary entries • Short biographies **Skills / strategies:** • Understand idioms and expressions • Relate to personal experience • Classify vocabulary using context • Critical thinking	**Task:** • Write a college application essay **Skill:** • Restrictive and non-restrictive adjective clauses
• Ask <u>Is something wrong?</u> to express concern about someone's state of mind. • Ask <u>What's going on?</u> to show interest in the details of someone's problem. • Begin an explanation with <u>Well, basically</u> to characterize a problem in few words. • Say <u>Hang in there</u> to offer support to someone facing a difficulty. • Say <u>Anytime</u> to acknowledge someone's appreciation and minimize what one has done.	**Listening Skills:** • Listen to predict • Listen to activate parts of speech • Listen for details • Listen to retell a story • Listen to summarize **PRONUNCIATION BOOSTER** • Vowel reduction to /ə/	**Texts:** • A self-test about how fearful you are • Interview responses about how fear affects people physically • An article about Marlee Matlin • Profiles of three heroes **Skills / strategies:** • Understand idioms and expressions • Understand meaning from context • Summarize	**Task:** • Write a short report about a dangerous or frightening event **Skill:** • Reducing adverbial clauses
• Introduce an uncomfortable topic with <u>there's something I need to bring up</u>. • Say <u>I didn't realize that</u> to acknowledge a complaint about your behavior. • Use <u>I didn't mean to …</u> to apologize for and summarize someone's complaint. • Say <u>On the contrary</u> to assure someone that you don't feel the way they think you might. • Say <u>I can see your point</u> to acknowledge someone's point of view.	**Listening Skills:** • Listen to activate grammar • Listen to summarize the main idea • Listen to infer information • Listen to draw conclusions **PRONUNCIATION BOOSTER** • Shifting emphatic stress	**Texts:** • Profiles about people's shortcomings • Descriptions of different workshops • An article on friendship **Skills / strategies:** • Understand idioms and expressions • Understand meaning from context • Apply ideas • Relate to personal experience	**Task:** • Write a three-paragraph essay presenting a solution to a common shortcoming **Skill:** • Transitional topic sentences
• Exclaim <u>You've got to see this</u>! to urge someone to look at something. • Introduce a statement with <u>Seriously</u> to insist someone not hesitate to take your suggestion. • Say <u>That's priceless</u> to strongly praise something. • Agree informally with <u>Totally</u>.	**Listening Skills:** • Listen to activate vocabulary • Listen to summarize • Listen to take notes • Listen to apply ideas **PRONUNCIATION BOOSTER** • Intonation of sarcasm	**Texts:** • A self-test about your sense of humor • An article about the health benefits of laughter • An article about the theories of humor • Descriptions of practical jokes **Skills / strategies:** • Understand idioms and expressions • Critical thinking • Classify	**Task:** • Write a true or imaginary story **Skill:** • Writing dialogue

UNIT	COMMUNICATION GOALS	VOCABULARY	GRAMMAR
UNIT 6 **Troubles While Traveling** PAGE 62	• Describe some causes of travel hassles • Express gratitude for a favor while traveling • Discuss staying safe on the Internet • Talk about lost, stolen, or damaged property	• Travel nouns **Word Study:** • Past participles as noun modifiers	• Unreal conditional sentences: continuous forms • Unreal conditional statements with <u>if it weren't for</u> … / <u>if it hadn't been for</u> … **GRAMMAR BOOSTER** • The conditional: summary and extension
UNIT 7 **Mind Over Matter** PAGE 74	• Suggest that someone is being gullible • Examine superstitions for believability • Talk about the power of suggestion • Discuss phobias	• Ways to express disbelief • Expressions with <u>mind</u> **Word Study:** • Noun and adjective forms	• Nouns: indefinite, definite, unique, and generic meaning (review and expansion) • Indirect speech: <u>it</u> + a passive reporting verb **GRAMMAR BOOSTER** • Article usage: summary • Definite article: additional uses • More non-count nouns with both a countable and an uncountable sense • Grammar for Writing: indirect speech with passive reporting verbs
UNIT 8 **Performing at Your Best** PAGE 86	• Discuss your talents and strengths • Suggest ways to boost intelligence • Explain how you produce your best work • Describe what makes someone a "genius"	• Expressions to describe talents and strengths • Adjectives that describe aspects of intelligence	• Using auxiliary <u>do</u> for emphatic stress • The subjunctive **GRAMMAR BOOSTER** • Grammar for Writing: emphatic stress • Infinitives and gerunds in place of the subjunctive
UNIT 9 **What Lies Ahead?** PAGE 98	• Discuss the feasibility of future technologies • Evaluate applications of innovative technologies • Discuss how to protect our future environment • Examine future social and demographic trends	• Innovative technologies • Ways to express a concern about consequences • Describing social and demographic trends	• The passive voice: the future, the future as seen from the past, and the future perfect • The passive voice in unreal conditional sentences **GRAMMAR BOOSTER** • Grammar for Writing: when to use the passive voice
UNIT 10 **An Interconnected World** PAGE 110	• React to news about global issues • Describe the impact of foreign imports • Discuss the pros and cons of globalization • Suggest ways to avoid culture shock	• Phrasal verbs to discuss issues and problems	• Separability of transitive phrasal verbs **GRAMMAR BOOSTER** • Phrasal verbs: expansion

What is *Summit?*

Summit is a two-level high-intermediate to advanced communicative course that develops confident, culturally fluent English speakers able to navigate the social, travel, and professional situations they will encounter as they use English in their lives. *Summit* can follow the intermediate level of any communicative series, including the four-level *Top Notch* course.

Summit delivers immediate, demonstrable results in every class session through its proven pedagogy and systematic and intensive recycling of language. Each goal- and achievement-based lesson is tightly correlated to the Can-Do Statements of the Common European Framework of Reference (CEFR). The course is fully benchmarked to the Global Scale of English (GSE).

Each level of *Summit* contains material for 60 to 90 hours of classroom instruction. Its full array of additional print and digital components can extend instruction to 120 hours if desired. Furthermore, the entire *Summit* course can be tailored to blended learning with its integrated online component, *MyEnglishLab*. *Summit* offers more ready-to-use teacher resources than any other course available today.

NEW This third edition represents a major revision of content and has a greatly increased quantity of exercises, both print and digital. Following are some key new features:

- **Conversation Activator Videos** to build communicative competence
- **Discussion Activator Videos** to increase quality and quantity of expression
- A **Test-Taking Skills Booster** (and **Extra Challenge Reading Activities**) to help students succeed in the reading and listening sections of standardized tests
- An **Understand Idioms and Expressions** section in each unit increases the authenticity of student spoken language

Award-Winning Instructional Design*

Demonstrable confirmation of progress

Every two-page lesson has a clearly stated communication goal and culminates in a guided conversation, free discussion, debate, presentation, role play, or project that achieves the goal. Idea framing and notepadding activities lead students to confident spoken expression.

Cultural fluency

Summit audio familiarizes students with a wide variety of native and non-native accents. Discussion activities reflect the topics people of diverse cultural backgrounds talk about in their social and professional lives.

Explicit vocabulary and grammar

Clear captioned illustrations and dictionary-style presentations, all with audio, take the guesswork out of meaning and ensure comprehensible pronunciation. Grammar is embedded in context and presented explicitly for form, meaning, and use. The unique "Recycle this Language" feature encourages active use of newly learned words and grammar during communication practice.

Active listening syllabus

More than 50 listening tasks at each level of *Summit* develop critical thinking and crucial listening comprehension skills such as listen for details, main ideas, confirmation of content, inference, and understand meaning from context.

Summit is the recipient of the Association of Educational Publishers' Distinguished Achievement Award.

Conversation and Discussion Activators

Memorable conversation models with audio provide appealing natural social language and conversation strategies essential for post-secondary learners. Rigorous Conversation Activator and Discussion Activator activities with video systematically stimulate recycling of social language, ensuring it is not forgotten. A unique Pronunciation Booster provides lessons and interactive practice, with audio, so students can improve their spoken expression.

Systematic writing skills development

Summit teaches the conventions of correct English writing so students will be prepared for standardized tests, academic study, and professional communication. Lessons cover key writing and rhetorical skills such as using parallel structure and avoiding sentence fragments, run-on sentences, and comma splices. Intensive work in paragraph and essay development ensures confident and successful writing.

Reading skills and strategies

Each unit of *Summit* builds critical thinking and key reading skills and strategies such as paraphrasing, drawing conclusions, expressing and supporting an opinion, and activating prior knowledge. Learners develop analytical skills and increase fluency while supporting their answers through speaking.

*We wish you and your students enjoyment and success with **Summit**. We wrote it for you.*
Joan Saslow and Allen Ascher

ActiveTeach

Maximize the impact of your *Summit* lessons. Digital Student's Book pages with access to all audio and video provide an interactive classroom experience that can be used with or without an interactive whiteboard (IWB). It includes a full array of easy-to-access digital and printable features.

For class presentation . . .

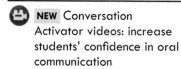 **NEW** Conversation Activator videos: increase students' confidence in oral communication

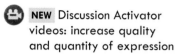 **NEW** Discussion Activator videos: increase quality and quantity of expression

 **NEW** Extra Grammar Exercises: ensure mastery of grammar

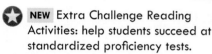 **NEW** Extra Challenge Reading Activities: help students succeed at standardized proficiency tests.

PLUS

- Interactive Whiteboard tools, including zoom, highlight, links, notes, and more.
- Clickable Audio: instant access to the complete classroom audio program
- *Summit TV* Video Program: fully-revised authentic TV documentaries as well as unscripted on-the-street interviews, featuring a variety of regional and non-native accents

For planning . . .

- A *Methods Handbook* for a communicative classroom
- Detailed timed lesson plans for each two-page lesson
- *Summit TV* teaching notes
- Complete answer keys, audio scripts, and video scripts

For extra support . . .

- Hundreds of extra printable activities, with teaching notes
- *Summit TV* activity worksheets

For assessment . . .

- Ready-made unit and review achievement tests with options to edit, add, or delete items.

Ready-made Summit Web Projects provide authentic application of lesson language.

MyEnglishLab

An optional online learning tool

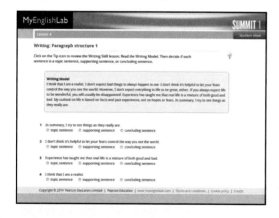

- **NEW** Immediate, meaningful feedback on wrong answers
- **NEW** Remedial grammar exercises
- **NEW** Grammar Coach videos for general reference
- Interactive practice of all material presented in the course
- Grade reports that display performance and time on task
- Auto-graded achievement tests

Workbook

Lesson-by-lesson written exercises to accompany the Student's Book

Full-Course Placement Tests

Choose printable or online version

Classroom Audio Program

- A set of Audio CDs, as an alternative to the clickable audio in ActiveTeach
- Contains a variety of authentic regional and non-native accents to build comprehension of diverse English speakers
- **NEW** The app *Summit Go* allows access anytime, anywhere and lets students practice at their own pace. The entire audio program is also available for students at www.english.com/summit3e.

Teacher's Edition and Lesson Planner

- Detailed interleaved lesson plans, language and culture notes, answer keys, and more
- Also accessible in digital form in ActiveTeach

For more information: www.pearsonelt.com/summit3e

ABOUT THE AUTHORS

Joan Saslow

Joan Saslow has taught in a variety of programs in South America and the United States. She is author or coauthor of a number of widely used courses, some of which are *Ready to Go*, *Workplace Plus*, *Literacy Plus*, and *Top Notch*. She is also author of *English in Context*, a series for reading science and technology. Ms. Saslow was the series director of *True Colors* and *True Voices*. She has participated in the English Language Specialist Program in the U.S. Department of State's Bureau of Educational and Cultural Affairs.

Allen Ascher

Allen Ascher has been a teacher and teacher trainer in China and the United States, as well as academic director of the intensive English program at Hunter College. Mr. Ascher has also been an ELT publisher and was responsible for publication and expansion of numerous well-known courses including *True Colors*, *NorthStar*, the *Longman TOEFL Preparation Series*, and the *Longman Academic Writing Series*. He is coauthor of *Top Notch*, and he wrote the "Teaching Speaking" module of *Teacher Development Interactive*, an online multimedia teacher-training program.

Ms. Saslow and Mr. Ascher are frequent presenters at professional conferences and have been coauthoring courses for teens, adults, and young adults since 2002.

AUTHORS' ACKNOWLEDGMENTS

The authors wish to thank Katherine Klagsbrun for developing the digital Extra Challenge Reading Activities that appear with all reading selections in **Summit 2**.

The authors are indebted to these reviewers, who provided extensive and detailed feedback and suggestions for **Summit**, as well as the hundreds of teachers who completed surveys and participated in focus groups.

Cris Asperti, CEL LEP, São Paulo, Brazil • **Diana Alicia Ávila Martínez**, CUEC, Monterrey, Mexico • **Shannon Brown**, Nagoya University of Foreign Studies, Nagoya, Japan • **Cesar Byrd**, Universidad ETAC Campus Chalco, Mexico City, Mexico • **Maria Claudia Campos de Freitas**, Metalanguage, São Paulo, Brazil • **Alvaro Del Castillo Alba**, CBA, Santa Cruz, Bolivia • **Isidro Castro Galván**, Instituto Teocalli, Monterrey, Mexico • **Melisa Celi**, Idiomas Católica, Lima, Peru • **Carlos Celis**, CEL LEP, São Paulo, Brazil • **Jussara Costa e Silva**, Prize Language School, São Paulo, Brazil • **Inara Couto**, CEL LEP, São Paulo, Brazil • **Gemma Crouch**, ICPNA Chiclayo, Peru • **Ingrid Valverde Diaz del Olmo**, ICPNA Cusco, Peru • **Jacqueline Díaz Esquivel**, PROULEX, Guadalajara, Mexico • **María Eid Ceneviva**, CBA, Cochabamba, Bolivia • **Erika Licia Esteves Silva**, Murphy English, São Paulo, Brazil • **Cristian Garay**, Idiomas Católica, Lima, Peru • **Miguel Angel Guerrero Pozos**, PROULEX, Guadalajara, Mexico • **Anderson Francisco Guimarães Maia**, Centro Cultural Brasil Estados Unidos, Belém, Brazil • **Cesar Guzmán**, CAADI Monterrey, Mexico • **César Iván Hernández Escobedo**, PROULEX, Guadalajara, Mexico • **Robert Hinton**, Nihon University, Tokyo, Japan • **Segundo**

Huanambal Díaz, ICPNA Chiclayo, Peru • **Chandra Víctor Jacobs Sukahai**, Universidad de Valle de México, Monterrey, Mexico • **Yeni Jiménez Torres**, Centro Colombo Americano Bogotá, Colombia • **Simon Lees**, Nagoya University of Foreign Studies, Nagoya, Japan • **Thomas LeViness**, PROULEX, Guadalajara, Mexico • **Amy Lewis**, Waseda University, Tokyo, Japan • **Luz Libia Rey**, Centro Colombo Americano, Bogotá, Colombia • **Diego López**, Idiomas Católica, Lima, Peru • **Junior Lozano**, Idiomas Católica, Lima, Peru • **Tanja McCandie**, Nanzan University, Nagoya, Japan • **Tammy Martínez Nieves**, Universidad Autónoma de Nuevo León, Monterrey, Mexico • **María Teresa Meléndez Mantilla**, ICPNA Chiclayo, Peru • **Mónica Nomberto**, ICPNA Chiclayo, Peru • **Otilia Ojeda**, Monterrey, Mexico • **Juana Palacios**, Idiomas Católica, Lima, Peru • **Giuseppe Paldino Mayorga**, Jellyfish Learning Center, San Cristobal, Ecuador • **Henry Eduardo Pardo Lamprea**, Universidad Militar Nueva Granada, Colombia • **Dario Paredes**, Centro Colombo Americano, Bogotá, Colombia • **Teresa Noemí Parra Alarcón**, Centro Anglo Americano de Cuernavaca, S.C., Cuernavaca, Mexico • **Carlos Eduardo de la Paz Arroyo**, Centro Anglo Americano de Cuernavaca, S.C.,

Cuernavaca, Mexico • **José Luis Pérez Treviño**, Instituto Obispado, Monterrey, Mexico • **Evelize Maria Plácido Florian**, São Paulo, Brazil • **Armida Rivas**, Monterrey, Mexico • **Luis Rodríguez Amau**, ICPNA Chiclayo, Peru • **Fabio Ossaamn Rok Kaku**, Prize Language School, São Paulo, Brazil • **Ana María Román Villareal**, CUEC, Monterrey, Mexico • **Reynaldo Romano C.**, CBA, La Paz, Bolivia • **Francisco Rondón**, Centro Colombo Americano, Bogotá, Colombia • **Peter Russell**, Waseda University, Tokyo, Japan • **Rubena St. Louis**, Universidad Simón Bolivar, Caracas, Venezuela • **Marisol Salazar**, Centro Colombo Americano, Bogotá, Colombia • **Miguel Sierra**, Idiomas Católica, Lima, Peru • **Greg Strong**, Aoyama Gakuin University, Tokyo, Japan • **Gerald Talandis**, Toyama University, Toyama, Japan • **Stephen Thompson**, Nagoya University of Foreign Studies, Nagoya, Japan • **José Luis Urbina Hurtado**, Instituto Tecnológico de León, Mexico • **René F. Valdivia Pereyra**, CBA, Santa Cruz, Bolivia • **Magno Alejandro Vivar Hurtado**, Salesian Polytechnic University, Ecuador • **Belkis Yanes**, Caracas, Venezuela • **Holger Zamora**, ICPNA Cusco, Peru • **Maria Cristina Zanon Costa**, Metalanguage, São Paulo, Brazil • **Kathia Zegarra**, Idiomas Católica, Lima, Peru.

UNIT 6
Troubles While Traveling

COMMUNICATION GOALS

1 Describe some causes of travel hassles
2 Express gratitude for a favor while traveling
3 Discuss staying safe on the Internet
4 Talk about lost, stolen, or damaged property

PREVIEW

A FRAME YOUR IDEAS Read about the online contest. On a separate sheet of paper, write your own tips for the common travel hassles.

THE PRACTICAL TRAVELER

HATE TRAVEL HASSLES? ENTER THE TRAVEL TIPS CONTEST!

CONTEST DIRECTIONS: Click on a pull-down menu to enter your own tip for dealing with a specific travel hassle. When you have finished entering all your tips, click on the link to our secure server to submit your tips. Contest winner will be announced on July 15. All decisions final.

CONTEST DEADLINE: July 1

Click here for a full list of prizes for the finalists.

No limit on number of submissions. Enter as many times as you want!

AIR TRAVEL

Inedible or no food on flights ▾
Unexpected checked baggage fees ▾
Carry-on luggage fees ▾
Insufficient room in overhead bins ▾
Overbooked flights ▾
Missed connections ▾
Lost luggage ▾
Long lines at check-in and security screening ▾
Items confiscated by security ▾

CAR TRAVEL

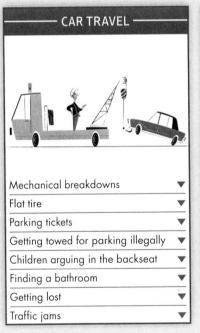

Mechanical breakdowns ▾
Flat tire ▾
Parking tickets ▾
Getting towed for parking illegally ▾
Children arguing in the backseat ▾
Finding a bathroom ▾
Getting lost ▾
Traffic jams ▾

OTHER TRAVEL HASSLES

Poor air-conditioning or heating ▾
No phone service or Wi-Fi access ▾
Delays ▾
Unexpected bus or train delays ▾
Uncomfortable seats ▾
Dirty bathrooms ▾
Loud or rude passengers ▾

CONTINUE ❯   SUBMIT ❯

B ▶3:16 VOCABULARY TRAVEL NOUNS Find and circle these words and phrases in the contest. Listen and repeat. Then, with a partner, explain the meaning of each one.

checked baggage fees   security screening
carry-on luggage   a breakdown
an overhead bin   a flat tire
a missed connection   a parking ticket

C DISCUSSION Share your tips. Decide which tips you think are good enough to win the contest.

D ▶ 3:17 **SPOTLIGHT** Read and listen to two friends talking about a travel hassle on a business trip. Notice the spotlighted language.

Edison: Oh, no. My folder's missing! It had my passport and my boarding pass in it.

Yuji: Uh-oh! Try to think. When did you see it last? Was it at the hotel?

Edison: Let's see … **I'm drawing a blank.** Oh! I remember now. I'd just finished printing out the boarding pass when the front desk called to say the airport limo was waiting downstairs. So I got my stuff together and split.

Yuji: Do you think you could have left the folder in the room or at the front desk when you checked out? Or what about in the limo?

Edison: Well, I distinctly remember looking back at the seat of the limo before I slammed the door, just to check that I hadn't left anything, and I hadn't. It's got to be in the hotel.

Yuji: Well, don't freak out. **It's a safe bet** they'll find it in the hotel.

Edison: You know, if I hadn't been rushing for the limo, this wouldn't have happened. **The way I see it,** I have no choice but to go back to the hotel. I'll grab a cab outside. You go on. You need to catch that plane.

Yuji: OK.

Edison: But if that folder isn't at the hotel, **I'm toast.** If it weren't for my stupid mistake, I wouldn't be going through this hassle. What'll happen if I miss the dinner?

Yuji: Well, **you'll cross that bridge when you come to it.** But hey, **no sweat.** If the folder's there, you can be back in time to make the four o'clock. We can meet up later. The dinner's not till seven.

Edison: OK. **I'm off.** Keep your fingers crossed!

E **UNDERSTAND IDIOMS AND EXPRESSIONS** Match the expressions from Spotlight with the statement or phrase that has a similar meaning.

1 I'm drawing a blank.

2 It's a safe bet.

3 the way I see it

4 I'm toast.

5 You'll cross that bridge when you come to it.

6 No sweat.

7 I'm off.

a Don't worry about it.

b It's very probable.

c I'm in big trouble.

d You can worry about that later.

e I can't remember.

f I'm leaving right now.

g in my opinion

F **THINK AND EXPLAIN** What do you think the outcome of the situation will be? What are Edison's options if the folder isn't found in his room or at the front desk? Explain.

SPEAKING Check hassles you've experienced and write details about when and where they happened. Then discuss with a partner.

My Experiences	Details
☐ I lost my passport.	
☐ I missed a plane / bus / train.	
☐ I missed a connecting flight.	
☐ My luggage was delayed or lost.	
☐ My car got towed.	
☐ I was in a vehicle that broke down.	
☐ I got a parking ticket.	
☐ My cosmetics were confiscated at security.	
☐ Other	

LESSON 1

GOAL Describe some causes of travel hassles

A ▶3:18 **GRAMMAR SPOTLIGHT** Read the interviews about travel hassles. Notice the spotlighted grammar.

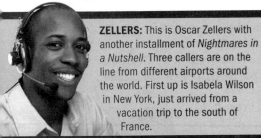

ZELLERS: This is Oscar Zellers with another installment of *Nightmares in a Nutshell.* Three callers are on the line from different airports around the world. First up is Isabela Wilson in New York, just arrived from a vacation trip to the south of France.

ZELLERS: Ms. Wilson, I understand you had your perfume taken from you when you went through security.

❶ WILSON: Unfortunately, yes. I got to the airport late and had to take my bag through security. But I'd forgotten the *expensive* French perfume I'd packed in that bag. It's not as if I don't know you can't take liquids through security. If I**'d been thinking** clearly, I **would have arrived** early enough to check my bag. Can you believe it was confiscated?!

ZELLERS: Next up is James Robillard in Montreal. He arrived in Brazil yesterday with an expired business visa and was put on a return flight back to Montreal. How unfortunate, Mr. Robillard!

❷ ROBILLARD: You can say that again! But frankly I'm pretty annoyed that the agent here in Montreal who checked me in didn't notice the expired visa. If she**'d been paying** better attention—instead of worrying about how much my baggage weighed!—she **would have noticed** it. She simply **couldn't have been looking for** the expiration date on the visa. She took a quick glance and saw that my passport was valid, but that was it.

ZELLERS: And last but not least, let's talk to Alice Yang. Ms. Yang started out in Shanghai and flew to Los Angeles, where she connected with her flight to San Salvador. But Ms. Yang's checked luggage wasn't transferred to the San Salvador flight. What bad luck, Ms. Yang!

❸ YANG: It sure was. And I've only got one day here in El Salvador. Tomorrow I'm departing for Bolivia, then the next day, Ecuador, then Peru! My bags may never catch up with me. You know, if I **were traveling** on a weekday, or if I had another day here, it **wouldn't be** such a problem since I could go shopping, but today is Sunday and most stores are closed. Take it from me. If you **have to change** planes, don't even think of checking your bag. Better safe than sorry!

B **DISCUSSION** Whose situation would be the most frustrating for you? Explain.

 C **GRAMMAR** UNREAL CONDITIONAL SENTENCES: CONTINUOUS FORMS

Use continuous verb forms in unreal conditional sentences to express actions in progress.

Present unreal conditional sentences

You can use <u>were</u> (or <u>weren't</u>) + a present participle in the <u>if</u> clause. You can use <u>would be</u> (or <u>wouldn't be</u>) + a present participle in the result clause. Note: The verb forms should reflect what you want to express. You don't have to use continuous forms in both clauses.

> If I **were walking** in traffic, I **wouldn't be talking** on my cell phone.
> [continuous forms in both clauses]
> If he walked there, he **would be going** through the most dangerous section of town.
> [continuous form only in the result clause]

Past unreal conditional sentences

You can use <u>had been</u> (or <u>hadn't been</u>) + a present participle in the <u>if</u> clause. You can use <u>would have been</u> (or <u>wouldn't have been</u>) + a present participle in the result clause. You don't have to use continuous forms in both clauses.

> If he**'d been using** his webcam during the conference call, he **would have been wearing** a tie.
> [continuous forms in both clauses]
> If I **hadn't been checking** my messages, I wouldn't have known the flight was delayed. [continuous form only in the <u>if</u> clause]

Sequence of tenses

The traditional sequence of tenses in all past unreal conditional sentences (past perfect in the <u>if</u> clause and <u>would have</u> + a past participle in the result clause) can change to express time. Compare the following sentences.

past unreal condition	present or past result
If I**'d gone** to India last year,	I **wouldn't be flying** there right now.
If I**'d gone** to India last year,	I **would have seen** the Taj Mahal.

Remember:
Conditional sentences usually have two clauses: an if (or "condition") clause and a result clause. The clauses in conditional sentences can be reversed.

Real (or "factual") conditionals describe the results of real conditions. Unreal conditionals describe the results of unreal conditions.

Be careful! Don't use <u>would</u> in the <u>if</u> clause in any unreal conditional sentence.

> If I were watching TV, I would be watching the news.
> NOT If I ~~would be watching~~ TV, …

GRAMMAR BOOSTER p. 137
The conditional: summary and extension

D **UNDERSTAND THE GRAMMAR**   Choose the sentence that best explains the meaning of each quotation. Then, with a partner, make a statement with <u>should have</u> to indicate what could have prevented the problem.

> ❝I should have made the reservation for the right date.❞

1 "If the reservation had been made for the right date, I wouldn't be waiting for a standby seat now."
   a The reservation was made for the right date, so I won't have to wait for a standby seat.
   b The reservation was made for the wrong date, so I'm waiting for a standby seat now.
   c The reservation wasn't made for the right date, so I don't have to wait for a standby seat.

2 "If my sister had been watching her bags, they wouldn't have gotten stolen."
   a My sister wasn't watching her bags, so they got stolen.
   b My sister isn't watching, so they might get stolen.
   c My sister was watching her bags, so they didn't get stolen.

3 "I wouldn't have missed the announcement if I hadn't been streaming a movie."
   a I was streaming a movie, and it caused me to miss the announcement.
   b I wasn't streaming a movie, so I didn't miss the announcement.
   c I wasn't streaming a movie, but I missed the announcement anyway.

E **GRAMMAR PRACTICE**   Circle the correct verb phrase to complete each statement.

1 If you (would be / were) at the hotel now, you (would be / would have been) sleeping.

2 If we (had / would have) packed more carefully, we (wouldn't be / wouldn't have been) paying these exorbitant overweight baggage fees!

3 They could (take / have taken) the three o'clock flight if they (would have been / had been) watching the departure board.

4 Karina (would be / would have been) wearing her most comfortable shoes on the tour today if they (wouldn't have been / weren't) sitting in her lost luggage right now.

5 If they (hadn't / wouldn't have) been speeding, they wouldn't (get / have gotten) that ticket.

F **PAIR WORK**   With a partner, take turns completing the unreal conditional sentences, using continuous verb forms.

1 If it were Monday, I ....*would be walking to work right now*.... .

2 I would have been late to class if ....

3 We would be watching the game now if ....

4 If I were at home, I ....

5 There's no way I would have missed the train if ....

NOW YOU CAN   Describe some causes of travel hassles

A **NOTEPADDING**   Write two travel hassles you or someone you know has faced. Write a statement with <u>should have</u> about how you could have avoided the hassle. Use the chart on page 63 for ideas.

What happened?	How could it have been avoided?
My brother's car got towed last May in New York.	He should have been paying attention to the signs.

What happened?	How could it have been avoided?

 B **DISCUSSION ACTIVATOR**   Discuss the travel hassles you experienced. Make at least one statement in the unreal conditional about how you could have avoided the hassle. Say as much as you can.

> ❝If I hadn't been listening to a podcast, I wouldn't have missed the flight announcement.❞

LESSON 2 · GOAL Express gratitude for a favor while traveling

A GRAMMAR   UNREAL CONDITIONAL STATEMENTS WITH <u>IF IT WEREN'T FOR</u> … / <u>IF IT HADN'T BEEN FOR</u> …

Make a present or past unreal conditional statement with <u>if it weren't for</u> / <u>if it hadn't been for</u> + an object to state an outcome that would occur or would have occurred under other circumstances. It's common to use this structure to express regret or relief.

Regret

"**If it weren't for** the traffic, we **would be** at the airport by now."
(= Under other circumstances, we would be at the airport by now, but unfortunately the traffic caused us not to be. We regret this.)

"**If it hadn't been for** my bad grades in science, **I would have studied** medicine."
(= Under other circumstances, I would have studied medicine. Unfortunately, my bad grades in science prevented that. I regret this.)

Relief

"**If it weren't for** this five-hour nonstop flight, the entire trip **would take** ten hours."
(= Under other circumstances, the trip would take ten hours. Fortunately, this nonstop flight caused the trip to be shortened by five hours. I'm relieved about this.)

"**If it hadn't been for** your help this morning, we **would have missed** the train."
(= Under other circumstances, we would have missed the train. Fortunately, your help prevented our missing the train. We're relieved about this.)

> **Remember:** You can also express strong regret with <u>If only</u>. If only can be followed by <u>were</u> or the past perfect.
>
> **If only there weren't** so much traffic, we would be at the airport by now.
>
> **If only I had had** better grades in science, I would have studied medicine.

If it hadn't been for my GPS, I would have gotten hopelessly lost!

B FIND THE GRAMMAR   Find and underline a statement using <u>If it weren't for</u> or <u>If it hadn't been for</u> and the unreal conditional in Spotlight on page 63. Is it expressing regret or relief?

C ▶ 3:19 UNDERSTAND THE GRAMMAR   Listen to the conversations and infer whether the speakers are expressing regret or relief in each conditional statement.

1 .... 　　 3 .... 　　 5 ....

2 .... 　　 4 .... 　　 6 ....

D ▶ 3:20 LISTEN TO ACTIVATE GRAMMAR   Listen again. Complete the paraphrase of what happened, according to what you hear. Use <u>if it weren't for</u> or <u>if it hadn't been for</u>.

1 He might still be waiting for the bus .... Ben.

2 .... the fact that they saw the other car, they might have had an accident.

3 Millie would love to go on the tour .... her cold.

4 They might still be in line .... the fact that she speaks Spanish.

5 They wouldn't be late for the play .... the flat tire.

6 .... her thoughtlessness, she thinks they wouldn't have divorced.

E GRAMMAR PRACTICE   On a separate sheet of paper, rewrite each statement, using <u>if it weren't for</u> or <u>if it hadn't been for</u>.

1 Without this cold, I would go to the museum with you tomorrow.

2 I would have totally missed our appointment without the hotel wake-up call.

3 Without that announcement, we would have gone to the wrong departure gate.

4 We would have arrived two hours early without the airline's text message.

5 Without the flight attendant's help with this heavy bag, I would have gotten a backache trying to put it in the overhead bin.

F GRAMMAR PRACTICE First complete the statements with true information, using <u>if it weren't for</u> or <u>if it hadn't been for</u>. Then take turns reading your information with a partner.

1 I wouldn't speak English this well ....

2 I would [or wouldn't] have traveled outside of my country ....

3 I would [or wouldn't] be a great athlete ....

4 I would [or wouldn't] have gone out last night ....

NOW YOU CAN Express gratitude for a favor while traveling

A ▶3:21 **CONVERSATION SPOTLIGHT**
Read and listen. Notice the spotlighted conversation strategies.

A: Excuse me. **I wonder if you could do me a favor**.
B: No problem. **How can I help**?
A: I think I left my phone at the counter. Would you mind keeping my place in line?
B: Not at all. **I'd be happy to**.
A: Thanks. I'll be right back.
...
B: Well, that was fast! **It's a good thing** your phone was still there.
A: And if it hadn't been for you, I would have lost my place in line. Thanks!

TO GATE 2A

B ▶3:22 **RHYTHM AND INTONATION**
Listen again and repeat. Then practice the conversation with a partner.

C CONVERSATION ACTIVATOR
Create a similar conversation, using one of the pictures or another idea. Start like this: *Excuse me. I wonder if you could do me a favor...* Be sure to change roles and then partners.

... giving me a hand with this bag?

... keeping an eye on my things?

DON'T STOP!
• Explain why you need help.
• Explain the possible consequences of not getting help.
• Continue the conversation with small talk.
• Say as much as you can.

RECYCLE THIS LANGUAGE	
· No sweat.	· Don't freak out.
· I'm off.	· Anytime.
· Wish me luck!	

... grabbing that bag off the carousel?

... pointing me in the right direction?

GOAL Discuss staying safe on the Internet

A **READING WARM-UP** Do you use public Wi-Fi away from home? Why or why not?

B ▶ 3:23 **READING** Read about problems with public Wi-Fi. What surprised you the most?

USING PUBLIC WI-FI NETWORKS

So it's your first trip away from home, and you've got your smartphone, your tablet, or laptop with you, and you plan to keep up with everything and stay in touch while you're away. You're thinking, "No sweat. There are Wi-Fi hotspots everywhere, and it's free. Well, before you lull yourself into a false sense of security, consider the downside of all that free Wi-Fi.

If you connect to a public Wi-Fi network and send information through websites or mobile apps, it might be accessed by someone else who can, for example, use your credit information to make online purchases. OK. That's not the end of the world, you say, because an unusual buying pattern usually trips a "fraud alert" at the credit card company. They'll contact you, and you'll confirm you didn't make the purchase. The card will be canceled, limiting or preventing any damage, so no harm done.

But here's a downside: An imposter could use your e-mail account to impersonate you and scam people in your contact lists. In addition, a hacker could test your username and password to try to gain access to other websites—including sites that store your financial information.

Worst case scenario? Someone could actually steal your financial identity and pose as you to clean out your bank accounts, removing all your hard-earned money. Repairing a stolen identity can take a long time and cause a lot of hassle. Identity theft is no joke. Prevent it at all costs.

So beware: If you send e-mail, share digital photos and videos, use social networks, or bank online, you're sending personal information over the Internet. How to protect yourself? Think encryption. Encryption scrambles the information you send over the Internet into a code so it's unintelligible and therefore not accessible to others. If you're on a public wireless hotspot, send personal information only to sites that are fully encrypted, and avoid using any mobile apps that require personal or financial information.

And don't just assume a Wi-Fi hotspot is secure either. Most *don't* encrypt the information you send over the Internet and aren't secure. In fact, if a network doesn't require a WPA or WPA2 password, it's probably not secure, and your personal information, private documents, contacts, family photos, and even your log-in credentials (your username and password) for any site you enter could be up for grabs.

HOW TO TELL IF A WEBSITE IS ENCRYPTED

To determine if a website is encrypted, look for "https" at the start of the web address (the "s" is for "secure"). Some websites use encryption only on the sign-in page, but if any part of your session isn't encrypted, your entire account could be vulnerable. Look for "https" on every page you visit, not just when you sign in.

TIPS FOR USING WI-FI SECURELY

▶ Log in or send personal information only to websites you know are fully encrypted. If you find yourself on an unencrypted page, log out right away.

▶ Don't stay permanently signed in to an account. When you've finished using an account, log out.

▶ Do not use the same password on different websites. It could give someone who gains access to one of your accounts access to many of your accounts.

▶ For more control over when and how your device uses public Wi-Fi, consider changing your settings so your device doesn't connect automatically.

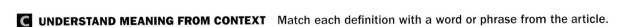

C **UNDERSTAND MEANING FROM CONTEXT** Match each definition with a word or phrase from the article.

...... **1** a person who fraudulently claims to be someone else

...... **2** the location on a website where you identify yourself in order to enter

...... **3** a general term for the username and password you use to identify yourself

...... **4** the disadvantage of something

...... **5** a warning that someone else might be using your credit card

...... **6** pretend to be someone else

...... **7** a place where one can access the Internet, usually for free

...... **8** the use of someone's financial information in order to steal

a a fraud alert

b identity theft

c impersonate

d an imposter

e log-in credentials

f a sign-in page

g downside

h a wireless hotspot

D PARAPHRASE On a separate sheet of paper, paraphrase each of the following statements from the article.

1 "An imposter could use your e-mail account to impersonate you and scam people in your contact lists."

> *A person could pretend to be you and trick people in your contact lists.*

2 "Before you lull yourself into a false sense of security, consider the downside of all that free Wi-Fi."

3 "Encryption scrambles the information you send over the Internet into a code so it's unintelligible and therefore not accessible to others."

4 "If a network doesn't require a WPA or WPA2 password, it's probably not secure, and your personal information, private documents, contacts, family photos, and even your login credentials … could be up for grabs."

5 "To determine if a website is encrypted, look for "https" at the start of the web address (the 's' is for 'secure')."

E FIND SUPPORTING DETAILS With a partner, discuss and answer the questions. Support your answers with information from the article.

1 What should you look for when sending information to a website when you're using a public Wi-Fi network?

2 How can you know whether a Wi-Fi network is secure?

3 What should you do after concluding your online banking when on a public Wi-Fi network?

4 What could happen if a hacker gained access to your contact list?

DIGITAL
EXTRA
CHALLENGE

5 What might happen if a credit card company discerns purchases on your card that are not ones you typically make?

NOW YOU CAN Discuss staying safe on the Internet

A FRAME YOUR IDEAS Complete the chart with what you do to stay secure on the Internet—at home or away.

	Always	Sometimes	Never
I use public Wi-Fi hotspots.	☐	☐	☐
I check to see if a website is encrypted.	☐	☐	☐
I use different passwords on different sites.	☐	☐	☐
I set my mobile device to automatically connect to nearby Wi-Fi.	☐	☐	☐
I protect myself against credit card fraud.	☐	☐	☐
I actively prevent my identity from being stolen.	☐	☐	☐

B GROUP WORK Compare your answers in a small group. Discuss which practices you were familiar with and which were new to you. Then add at least one other thing you do to keep yourself secure on the Internet.

> ❝ I change all my passwords once a week. I have a system for scrambling them that makes it easy for me to remember them. ❞

GOAL Talk about lost, stolen, or damaged property

DIGITAL STRATEGIES

A ▶3:24 **LISTENING WARM-UP** **WORD STUDY** **PAST PARTICIPLES AS NOUN MODIFIERS**
The past participles of transitive verbs can function as noun modifiers. They can precede or follow the noun they modify. Read and listen. Then listen again and repeat.

"My tire was **damaged**. I took my **damaged** tire to the garage."

"My purse was **stolen** at a store. I found the **stolen** purse (without my wallet!) at the back of the store."

"My passport was **lost**. Luckily, the police found the **lost** passport."

B **WORD STUDY PRACTICE 1** Choose five more past participles of transitive verbs from the chart on page 122. Write a sentence with each one, using the examples in Exercise A as a model.

C **WORD STUDY PRACTICE 2** On a separate sheet of paper, rewrite each sentence that contains an underlined object pronoun, using a participial adjective as a noun modifier.

1 When Julie took her skirt out of the closet, she saw that it was stained. She took <u>it</u> to the cleaners.

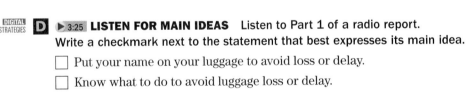

She took the stained skirt to the cleaners.

2 While we were at the train station, I found a pair of sunglasses that were lost. I gave <u>them</u> to the Lost and Found.

3 After walking up the steps to the pyramid, I noticed that the heel of my shoe was broken. The guy in the shoe repair stand fixed <u>it</u> in less than ten minutes.

PRONUNCIATION BOOSTER p. 147
· Regular past participle endings
· Reduction in perfect modals

4 We reported that our hotel room had been burglarized. The front desk sent someone to look at <u>it</u>.

5 The repair shop sells bargain suitcases that are damaged. It's a good deal because you can pay to have <u>them</u> repaired cheaply.

DIGITAL STRATEGIES

D ▶3:25 **LISTEN FOR MAIN IDEAS** Listen to Part 1 of a radio report. Write a checkmark next to the statement that best expresses its main idea.

☐ Put your name on your luggage to avoid loss or delay.

☐ Know what to do to avoid luggage loss or delay.

☐ Don't check bags that can be carried onto the plane.

Keep your copy of the luggage check in case your bag is lost or delayed.

E ▶3:26 **LISTEN TO CONFIRM CONTENT** Listen again. Write a checkmark next to the tips Tina Traveler gave listeners. Write an X next to any tips on the list she didn't give.

☐ 1 Put your address on your luggage inside and out.

☐ 2 Request reimbursement for toiletries if your baggage is delayed.

☐ 3 File a claim with your airline if your bags are lost.

☐ 4 Provide sales receipts to prove what you paid for the clothes in your lost luggage.

☐ 5 Don't put your prescription medicines in your checked bag.

☐ 6 Keep luggage checks for checked baggage in case you have to make a claim.

F ▶3:27 **LISTEN TO UNDERSTAND MEANING FROM CONTEXT**
Listen again and complete each statement with one of these words
or phrases from Tina Traveler's advice.

a claim	luggage checks
a connecting flight	receipts
depreciated	reimburse
an itinerary	toiletries

1 Cosmetics are an example of ....

2 The list of places and dates of your travel is ....

3 A value lower than the price you paid because the item isn't new is its .... value.

4 If you take two flights to get somewhere, the second one is called ....

5 Slips of paper showing the destination of your checked luggage are ....

6 Slips of paper showing what you paid for something you bought are ....

7 A form that records loss, delay, or damage to property is ....

8 If the airline pays you money to compensate you for a damaged bag, they .... you.

G ▶3:28 **LISTEN FOR DETAILS** Listen to Part 2 of Tina Traveler's report. Then answer the
questions. Listen again if necessary.

1 What is the Unclaimed Baggage Center?

2 What's the difference between the Unclaimed Baggage Center and
a Lost and Found office?

3 How many stores does the Center have?

4 Where does the Unclaimed Baggage Center get its merchandise?

5 How does it decide what to buy and what not to buy?

6 What does the center do before selling merchandise?

7 What does it do with merchandise it can't sell?

H **DISCUSSION** Would you shop at the Unclaimed Baggage Center?
Explain why or why not.

UNCLAIMED
BAGGAGE CENTER

NOW YOU CAN Talk about lost, stolen, or damaged property

A **NOTEPADDING** Write notes about a time your property was lost, stolen, or damaged when you
were traveling. Use words and phrases from Exercise F in your description if possible.

| when / where / what?: | 2016 / Orlando USA / guitar |
| **brief summary and outcome:** | The airline made me check my guitar. It wasn't transferred to my connecting |

flight in Panama. It was found and delivered to our hotel the next day.

| when / where / what?: | |
| **brief summary and outcome:** | |

B **DISCUSSION** Discuss the events you
wrote about on your notepad. Discuss what
happened to your property and what the
final outcome was. Respond to your partner.

❝ I freaked out when I didn't see the guitar case on
the carousel. If it hadn't been for the baggage
check, I would have been toast! ❞

❝ It's a good thing you saved that check! ❞

OPTIONAL WRITING Write about the event you
discussed. Include as many details as possible. Use the words
and phrases from Exercise F and other vocabulary from this unit.

A WRITING SKILL   Study the rules.

Choose one of these formats for organizing your supporting paragraphs when you want to compare and contrast places, objects, people, ideas, etc., in an essay. (Be sure to include expressions of comparison and contrast.)

Introductory paragraph
Begin with an introductory paragraph that says what you are going to compare and contrast.

Supporting paragraphs
Choose Format A or B to present and support your ideas.

Format A: Discuss the similarities in one paragraph and the differences in another.

Format B: Alternatively, you can focus on one specific aspect of the topic in each paragraph, and discuss the similarities and differences within each paragraph.

Concluding paragraph
Summarize your main ideas in a concluding paragraph.

WRITING MODEL

(Introductory paragraph)

Public and private transportation have both advantages and disadvantages, so it is fortunate to have options. To make a choice, you can take into account convenience, cost, destination, and the needs and tastes of the people you are traveling with. Other factors to consider are the length of the trip and (if it is important to you) the environmental impact of the means of transportation you choose.

(Format A)

Public and private transportation provide clear advantages for most people. They are similar in certain ways: Both are convenient and cut travel time, allowing people to travel farther to work or school. And with the exception of a bicycle, all vehicles used in public and private transportation are capable of providing a level of comfort available with modern technology, such as air-conditioning and heating.

On the other hand, public and private transportation are different in more ways than they are similar. Cars and bicycles offer a level of privacy and convenience not available in public transportation. You can make your own schedule, take a detour, and not have to pay fares or deal with people you don't want to be with. However, it is only with public transportation that you can move around, relax, and not have to pay attention to traffic or weather conditions.

OR

(Format B)

Regarding scheduling, private and public transportation are very different. When you travel by car, you can make your own schedule and stop when and where you want. Nevertheless, when you travel by bus or train you know exactly when you'll arrive, making planning easy.

In terms of comfort, private transportation has the clear advantage. Public transportation may be crowded and …

(Concluding paragraph)

Most people choose to use a mix of private and public transportation, depending on circumstances. However, if I could choose only one means of transportation, I'd go with the car. It has its disadvantages, but I like to travel alone or only with my family and to be able to make my own schedule. All in all, I'd say I'm a car person.

B APPLY THE WRITING SKILL   On a separate sheet of paper, write an essay comparing and contrasting two means of transportation. Include the paragraph types and formats shown in Exercise A. Use expressions of comparison and contrast.

Expressions to introduce comparisons and contrasts:	
Comparisons	**Contrasts**
Similarly,	While / Whereas …
Likewise,	Unlike …
By the same token,	Nonetheless,
In similar fashion,	Nevertheless,
… as well	In contrast,
… don't either	On the other hand,
	However,

SELF-CHECK

☐ Did I use expressions of comparison and contrast?

☐ Does my essay have an introductory and a concluding paragraph?

☐ Do the supporting paragraphs follow one of the formats illustrated above?

A ▶ 3:29 Listen to three conversations. On the notepad, summarize what happened in each conversation.

	Conversation Summary
1	
2	
3	

B Choose the correct verb phrase to complete each statement.

1 If it weren't for this long security line, I (will / would) get a cup of coffee.

2 If it hadn't been for the delay in my first flight, my checked bags (wouldn't miss / wouldn't have missed) the connection.

3 We wouldn't have had a flat tire if it (weren't / hadn't been) for all the broken glass on the road.

4 Martin would be here if it (weren't / wouldn't be) for this storm.

5 If it (weren't / wouldn't be) for my broken leg, I would be skiing right now.

C Replace the words or phrases that are crossed out in each statement with ones that make sense.

1 The compartment over your airline seat where you can place your suitcase is the ~~carousel~~.

2 Before you can board an airplane, you have to go through ~~a missed connection~~.

3 If you park in an illegal space, you might get a ~~flat tire~~ or, even worse, your car might get ~~a breakdown~~.

4 A ~~checked~~ bag is one that you take on board with you when you get on a flight.

D Choose the correct idiom or expression.

1 If you can't remember something you're sure you should be able to, you can say, "……"
  a I'm toast.   **b** I'm drawing a blank.

2 When you want to indicate you're about to leave, you can say, "……"
  a I'm off.   **b** I'll cross that bridge when I come to it.

3 If you want to reassure someone that a task won't be hard at all, you can say, "……"
  a No sweat.   **b** It's a good thing.

4 When you think something terrible is definitely going to happen, you can say, "……"
  a I'm off.   **b** I'm toast.

5 When you're sure you've concluded something correctly, you can say, "……"
  a I'm drawing a blank.   **b** It's a safe bet.

TEST-TAKING SKILLS BOOSTER p. 156

Web Project: Travel Nightmares
www.english.com/summit3e

COMMUNICATION GOALS
1 Suggest that someone is being gullible
2 Examine superstitions for believability
3 Talk about the power of suggestion
4 Discuss phobias

PREVIEW

A FRAME YOUR IDEAS Play the Illusion Game with a partner. Look at each image carefully for at least a minute. Do you both see the same thing?

The ILLUSION GAME

An illusion is something likely to be wrongly interpreted. Write an explanation of what the eye sees in each picture. Then compare your explanations with the ones below.

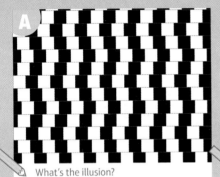

A

What's the illusion?

B

What's the illusion?

C

What's the illusion?

D

What's the illusion?

E

What's the illusion?

EXPLANATIONS **A** The horizontal lines appear to be sloping, creating uneven rows. But the lines actually are parallel. **B** We can see either two people or three objects that look like vases or chess pieces. **C** There are two zebras, but we only see one head. Depending on how we look at the image, the head appears to belong to the zebra on the left or to the one on the right. **D** We see half a man's face. Depending on how we look at it, he either appears to be looking out at us or in profile looking to the right. **E** The image appears to be moving, but it isn't.

B DISCUSSION What other things are we likely to misinterpret visually? What might cause us to misinterpret them?

❝Sometimes on a dark night, we might think we're seeing monsters, but in reality they're only trees. That illusion is caused by our imagination and our natural fear of the dark.❞

C ▶ 4:02 **SPOTLIGHT**   Read and listen to a conversation between two colleagues. Notice the spotlighted language.

Vicky: Tom, do you have a minute?

Tom: Sure, Vicky. Come on in and have a seat. **What's on your mind**?

Vicky: You know, **I may be imagining things**, but I have the distinct impression that my staff's either talking about me or has some kind of secret they don't want me to know about.

Tom: What gives you that impression?

Vicky: Well, for instance, for the last few days every time I get back from lunch, Bill and Emma and Ron are all huddled together in Emma's cubicle and talking, and the minute they realize I'm there, they shut up. I mean, that's not normal, is it? It makes me think they're talking about me behind my back.

Tom: Well, **if I were in your shoes**, I wouldn't automatically assume that.

Vicky: I sound paranoid, don't I? I mean, it sounds crazy to think it has something to do with *me*, right?

Tom: Not necessarily. Their behavior *does* seem to suggest they don't want you to know what they're talking about. **Keep in mind** that there may be a totally innocent explanation. Have you considered the possibility that maybe one of them's got a job offer, or that they're just gossiping? Hey! Who knows? Maybe they're gossiping about *me*!

Vicky: I suppose you're right.

Tom: **Don't get me wrong**. There's definitely something going on, but I wouldn't jump to any conclusions. *[phone rings]* I've got to take this. Just a sec … Well, as a matter of fact, she happens to be in my office right now. Why don't you all just walk over here, OK? … **The cat's out of the bag**, Vicky. We all know today's your birthday and we've been planning a little surprise celebration. The gang's got a cake and a little present for you. They're on their way over now.

Vicky: Oh, Tom. I feel like such an idiot!

D **UNDERSTAND IDIOMS AND EXPRESSIONS**   Find a spotlighted expression that expresses a similar meaning.

1 Please don't misunderstand me. ....

2 It's possible that what I'm thinking is an illusion. ....

3 Faced with the same situation as you, … ....

4 It's not a secret anymore. ....

5 Tell me what you're thinking about. ....

6 Don't forget … ....

E **THINK AND EXPLAIN**   Answer the questions with a partner. Explain your answers with information from Spotlight.

1 What makes Vicky think that her staff is talking about her behind her back?

2 Why is Vicky afraid that she sounds paranoid?

3 What does Tom mean when he says "there may be a totally innocent explanation"?

4 Did Tom know what Vicky's staff had been discussing?

SPEAKING   It is said that "seeing is believing," but can we trust our perceptions completely? Rank the following in order of reliability from **1** to **6**, with **1** being the most reliable. Provide examples.

☐	A news photograph on the Internet	☐	A claim made in an advertisement
☐	A story told by a friend	☐	Statistics cited by a politician
☐	A video documentary	☐	A witness's story about a miracle

GOAL | Suggest that someone is being gullible

A **GRAMMAR** NOUNS: INDEFINITE, DEFINITE, UNIQUE, AND GENERIC MEANING (REVIEW AND EXPANSION)

A noun (or noun phrase) is *indefinite* when it doesn't refer to a specific person, place, thing, or idea. Use the indefinite articles (<u>a</u> / <u>an</u>) with indefinite singular count nouns. Indefinite non-count nouns (for example, <u>music</u>, <u>love</u>) have no article.

> You can buy **a smart watch** if you like having everything at a glance. [indefinite, not a specific smart watch]

A noun (or noun phrase) is *definite* when it refers to a specific person, place, thing, or idea. An indefinite noun already mentioned becomes definite when mentioned a second time. Use the definite article (<u>the</u>) with definite singular and plural count nouns and with definite non-count nouns.

> **The wool** they used to make **the sweaters** in this store comes from Canada.
> [definite, specific wool and sweaters]
> I saw a movie last night. **The movie** was a documentary. [definite, second mention]

A count or non-count noun can represent a person, place, or thing that is *unique*; in other words, there's only one. Use <u>the</u>.

> **The president** has named two new foreign ministers.
> Some people claim climate change has no effect on **the environment**.

> **Remember:** Non-count nouns name things you cannot count. They are neither singular nor plural, but they always use a singular verb. Common categories of non-count nouns are abstract ideas, sports and activities, illnesses, academic subjects, and foods.

Count nouns can be used in a *generic* sense to represent all members of a class or group of people, places, or things. When using nouns in a generic sense, use a singular count noun with <u>a</u> / <u>an</u> or <u>the</u>, or use a plural count noun without an article. There is no difference in meaning.

> **A cat** is ⎫
> **The cat** is ⎬ a popular domestic pet in many countries of the world.
> **Cats** are ⎭

> **GRAMMAR BOOSTER** p. 138
> • Article usage: summary
> • Definite article: additional uses
> • More non-count nouns with both a countable and an uncountable sense

B **UNDERSTAND THE GRAMMAR** Read each statement and choose the phrase that describes the underlined word or phrase.

1 <u>Morning snow</u> makes highways dangerous.
  a refers to morning snow in general
  b refers to the snow that fell this morning

2 I think <u>animated movies</u> are boring.
  a refers to all animated movies
  b refers to some animated movies

3 <u>The present</u> they sent me was very expensive.
  a refers to a present as a member of a class
  b refers to a specific present I was sent

4 Some cultures regard <u>the shark</u> as a sign of luck.
  a refers to a specific shark we know about
  b refers to sharks as a class or group

5 <u>The queen</u> will address Parliament this week.
  a refers to a specific queen
  b refers to queens generically

6 <u>A queen</u> can address Parliament.
  a refers to a specific queen
  b refers to queens generically

C **GRAMMAR PRACTICE** Complete the statements about product claims. Insert <u>a</u>, <u>an</u>, or <u>the</u> before a noun or noun phrase where necessary. Write <u>X</u> if the noun shouldn't have an article.

1 .... British company claims to have invented .... machine that allows .... people to talk with their pets. .... company says .... machine, called the PetCom, will be available later in .... year.

2 It's well known that .... carrots are a good source of .... vitamins. In fact, ... research has determined that drinking .... glass of carrot juice every day can add .... years to your life.

3 .... WeightAway diet plan promises to help you lose .... weight fast. .... company guarantees that people following .... plan can lose up to 10 kilograms per week.

4 Last week, the news reported that thousands of people had sent .... money to .... organization advertising a shampoo that .... organization claimed would grow .... hair overnight.

A ► 4:03 **CONVERSATION SPOTLIGHT** Read and listen. Notice the spotlighted conversation strategies.

A: **Can you believe this**?
B: What?
A: This ad. It says, "Don't eat these three foods and lose all belly fat in one week! Guaranteed."
B: **Oh, come on**. You don't buy that, do you? **That's got to be** a total scam.
A: Of course it is. But people are gullible.
B: Why do they fall for stuff like that?
A: Wishful thinking, **I guess**. They believe what they want to be true.
B: **You can say that again.**

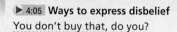

► 4:05 **Ways to express disbelief**
You don't buy that, do you?
That's just too good to be true.
No way can that be true.

B ► 4:04 **RHYTHM AND INTONATION** Listen again and repeat. Then practice the conversation with a partner.

C **CONVERSATION ACTIVATOR** Create a similar conversation, using the scams below. Start like this: *Can you believe this?* ... Be sure to change roles and then partners.

DON'T STOP!
- Explain why the message or ad is a scam.
- Speculate about why people might fall for it.
- Talk about other scams you've seen or heard about.
- Say as much as you can.

Extraordinary Space Age Investment Opportunity

Diamonds discovered in Mars rocks, just waiting to be mined!

Invest $1,000, receive at least $100,000 return on your investment

Act quickly. Spaceships leaving soon. Visit our website for more information

www.marsdiamonds.com

RICH QUICK

Using revolutionary 4-D printing technology, turn your garden dirt into genuine diamonds in just one month. No need to wait millennia!

Suddenly Happy

The Vinegar Diet Cure

Feeling Blue? Drink vinegar to cure depression in one short week

From: Prince Adebambo Boluwaji
Subject: Urgent Reply Needed

Most esteemed Sir:

Happy New Year!

With due respect and humility, I write to you. I know this message will come to you as a surprise. I am the next heir to the throne in Nigeria, the Crown Prince Adebambo Boluwaji. I am hoping that you will not disparage or betray my confident trust in your excellency after I propose to you for the mutual benefit of our families an investment in my government. I can assure you that the Treasury only needs a temporary loan and that if you deposit ONE MILLION U.S. DOLLARS into our national bank [account numbers below] I will personally deposit via electronic transfer TEN MILLION DOLLARS into your personal account in 60 days' time.

A ▶4:06 **GRAMMAR SPOTLIGHT** Read about some superstitions. Notice the spotlighted grammar.

Superstitious.com

A selection of superstitions from far and wide, then and now.

Good Luck

In some countries **it's said that** a frog brings good luck into the house it enters. (In others, however, **it's said that** this brings bad luck!) In Korea **it's believed that** dreaming about a pig will bring good luck because pigs symbolize wealth. Read more

Bad luck

In some cultures in the 18th century, when a worker died on the job, his shoes were brought to his house and placed on the table. Ever since, **it's been held that** putting shoes on a table is bad luck. There are other theories about the origin of this superstition, but they are all associated with bad luck and death. Read more

Weddings

In some cultures, **it's thought that** if the groom drops the wedding ring during the ceremony, the marriage is doomed. And in others, **it's said that** after the wedding, the spouse who goes to sleep first will be the first to die. Read more

Babies

In the past **it was said that** the sex of a baby could be predicted by suspending a wedding ring by a string over the palm of a pregnant woman. If the ring swung in a circle, the baby would be a girl. If it moved in a straight line, it would be a boy. Read more

Animals

It has been claimed that a dog eating grass brings rain and that rats leaving a ship signifies the ship will sink. Read more

Numbers

It's estimated that more than 80% of U.S. high-rise buildings don't have a 13th floor. This is because the number 13 is considered unlucky and building owners are afraid that few people would be willing to rent an apartment, hotel room, or office on the 13th floor. Read more

See more ▼

B **GROUP WORK** Are you familiar with any of the superstitions on superstitious.com? Do you know any other superstitions for the same categories? Compare information with your classmates.

C **GRAMMAR** **INDIRECT SPEECH: <u>IT</u> + A PASSIVE REPORTING VERB**

DIGITAL INDUCTIVE ACTIVITY

To report a generalized statement or belief, use <u>it</u> + a passive reporting verb + a noun clause. As in indirect speech, the verb in the noun clause reflects the tense of the reporting verb.

It is said that spilling salt **brings** bad luck.
It was widely **believed** that the storm **would be** terrible.
Before the election, **it had been asserted** that very few people **would come** out to vote.
It might be thought that the offer **is** a scam.
It used to be believed that changing bed sheets on a Friday **would bring** bad dreams.

Common reporting verbs

assert	feel
believe	hold
claim	say
estimate	think

Remember: You can also report generalized statements and beliefs with <u>people</u> or <u>they</u>:
  People [or **They**] **say** spilling salt brings bad luck.

GRAMMAR BOOSTER p. 140
Indirect speech with passive reporting verbs

D GRAMMAR PRACTICE Replace the subject and active verb in each statement with it + a passive reporting verb. Make necessary changes to the verb in the noun clause.

It is claimed
1 ~~They claim~~ that a pregnant woman at a funeral will bring bad luck.

2 People believe that lightning will never strike a house where a fire is burning.

3 They say if you hear thunder and the sound comes from your right side, then you can expect good luck.

4 They say that letting the first rain in May touch your face brings you luck throughout the year.

5 Some people hold that if you turn bread upside down after a slice has been cut from it, you will have bad luck.

6 They estimate that more than 50% of people in North America won't rent an apartment on the 13th floor.

> **PRONUNCIATION BOOSTER** p. 148
> Linking sounds

E PAIR WORK With a partner, discuss the six superstitions from Exercise D. Discuss whether you believe in any of them, and if so, why.

> ❝I totally disagree with the one about the pregnant woman at the funeral. I think a lot of superstitions about women are just sexist. ❞

F GRAMMAR PRACTICE On a separate sheet of paper, rewrite each passive statement in Exercise D, beginning with It used to be. Make necessary changes to the verb in the noun clause.

> 1 It used to be claimed that a pregnant woman at a funeral would bring bad luck.

NOW YOU CAN Examine superstitions for believability

A NOTEPADDING Ask three classmates about superstitions they have heard about or believe. Write the information on the notepad. Find out if they (or anyone they know) believe in them.

name: Ryan
superstition: If you break a mirror, you'll have seven years of bad luck.

name:
superstition:

name:
superstition:

name:
superstition:

Some ideas for categories of superstitions
- foods / drinks
- good luck / bad luck
- brides and grooms
- particular months, days, or dates
- particular numbers
- dreams
- death
- your own idea: ....

 DIGITAL VIDEO

B DISCUSSION ACTIVATOR Talk about the superstitions you listed on your notepad. Discuss why you or others believe (or don't believe) in them. Agree and disagree about the superstitions. Say as much as you can.

> **RECYCLE THIS LANGUAGE**
> - I think it's possible.
> - I agree / disagree.
> - People believe what they want to believe.
> - Oh, come on!
> - No way can that be true.
> - That's just wishful thinking.
> - Why do people fall for stuff like that?
> - Some people are just gullible.

A **READING WARM-UP** Do you think that your thoughts and beliefs can affect your health or the condition of your body? In what way?

DIGITAL
STRATEGIES   **B** ▶4:07 **READING** Read the article about placebos and nocebos. What do they have in common?

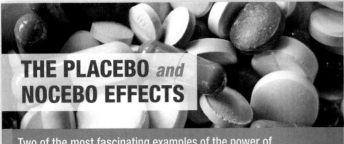

THE PLACEBO *and* NOCEBO EFFECTS

Two of the most fascinating examples of the power of suggestion in medicine are the *placebo effect* and the *nocebo effect*. These two opposite phenomena are two sides of the same coin. And while the placebo effect has been widely known for many years, the nocebo effect has been largely overlooked until recently and thus less well understood.

The word *placebo* refers to a fake medication (one that contains no active ingredients) or a medical procedure that patients believe will help them and then, as a result of that expectation, it does. In one well-known study, three groups of patients who were told they needed knee surgery underwent one of three procedures. One group had the usual standard surgery. In a second group, the knee was opened surgically but the interior was only washed. In the third group, the doctor made three tiny cuts in the skin, but didn't perform any surgery inside the knee at all. All patients believed they had had the standard surgery. At the end of a year, the patients who had had no surgery reported the same good results as those who had had the surgery.

It has been shown repeatedly that certain factors increase the effectiveness of placebos. If a pill, for example, looks like a genuine medicine, the person taking it is likely to believe it contains medicine. It has also been found that patients think larger pills contain larger doses of medicine, and thus must be more effective. Similarly, it has been demonstrated that taking two pills has a greater therapeutic effect than taking only one. Another important determiner of placebo effectiveness is the doctor-patient relationship. If the patient trusts the doctor administering the "medication," he or she is more likely to be helped or cured by it.

The nocebo effect is also based on the power of suggestion or expectation. If a patient has been told that a medication is likely to cause an adverse reaction (such as dizziness or headache), he or she is more likely to experience one. This has been demonstrated both in experiments and in actual medical practice. One dramatic non-medical experiment is often cited as an example of the nocebo effect: When given a non-alcoholic beverage that subjects were told was beer, they believed and acted as if they were drunk. They slurred their speech, acted silly, and even fell and hurt themselves. Simply believing a substance will make one drunk can result in drunkenness.

What are the implications of the placebo and nocebo effects for medical practice? Placebos can be used in research to help evaluate the effectiveness of real medications. If two groups of patients are treated with either a placebo or a real medication and both achieve the same result, it is clear that the medication lacks real effectiveness. Also, it is well known that some patients ask doctors for medications that are ineffective and potentially harmful (such as antibiotics for a common cold). Doctors can prescribe such patients a placebo, knowing that it may be effective and will cause no harm.

The nocebo effect, on the other hand, can present doctors with an ethical dilemma. Adverse reactions to particular medications are typically experienced by a very small percentage of patients. Doctors wonder if they should inform patients of these potential adverse reactions since they know they are very unlikely to occur. The power of suggestion of the nocebo effect could interfere with the more likely positive effects of a necessary medication, depriving patients of an effective treatment.

In conclusion, although we believe the body and the mind are separate, the existence of the placebo and nocebo effects suggests that the distinction between the two might be more complicated than we as yet understand. All humans are probably somewhat susceptible to the power of suggestion.

C **INFER MEANING** Choose the correct word or phrase to complete each statement.

1 Something that has escaped notice has been (investigated / overlooked).

2 The opposite of a placebo is a (fake / genuine) medicine.

3 (A placebo / An adverse reaction) is a harmful effect caused by taking a medication.

4 The false expectation that a substance is beer has been demonstrated to cause (silly behavior / an adverse reaction).

5 Antibiotics are an (effective / ineffective) medication for colds.

DRAW CONCLUSIONS Complete each statement, based on the information in the article.

1 The factor that doesn't contribute to the placebo effect is ....
  a the appearance of the medication
  b scientific research
  c trust in the doctor
  d the expectation that it will work

2 The knee surgery experiment demonstrates ....
  a the power of suggestion that surgery was performed
  b the value of washing the interior of the knee
  c the need for procedures in surgery
  d the harmful effects of fake procedures

3 The drunkenness experiment is an example of ....
  a the placebo effect
  b the nocebo effect
  c an ethical dilemma
  d the harmful effects of beer

4 ...... is one beneficial use of placebos.
  a The scientific evaluation of the effectiveness of new medications
  b The improvement of the doctor-patient relationship
  c Causing harmful adverse reactions
  d Reducing the cost of antibiotics

5 Under normal circumstances, adverse reactions to medications occur in ....
  a most patients
  b only a few patients
  c the sickest patients
  d the common cold

E **CRITICAL THINKING** Discuss the following questions.

1 What are the pros and cons of telling a patient about potential adverse reactions to a medication?

2 In what way are the placebo effect and the nocebo effect "two sides of the same coin"?

DIGITAL EXTRA CHALLENGE **3** In your opinion, are only gullible people susceptible to the placebo and nocebo effect? Explain.

NOW YOU CAN **Talk about the power of suggestion**

A **NOTEPADDING** Make a list of ways people are susceptible to the power of suggestion. Write what creates the suggestion and how it makes people behave or think.

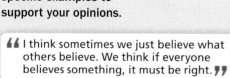
shampoo ads: seeing a beautiful model's hair makes people want to buy the shampoo

Some ideas
· advertisements
· celebrity behavior
· expert opinions
· superstitions
· sexism
· racism

 B **DISCUSSION** With a partner, discuss the information on your notepads, providing specific examples to support your opinions.

❝ I think sometimes we just believe what others believe. We think if everyone believes something, it must be right. ❞

RECYCLE THIS LANGUAGE	
· illusion	· What gives you that impression?
· scam	· I wouldn't jump to that conclusion.
· wishful thinking	· Not necessarily.
· claims	· Don't get me wrong.

OPTIONAL WRITING Write an essay of at least two paragraphs, describing two or three ways in which people are susceptible to the power of suggestion. Try to explain why it's hard to avoid being influenced by messages in the environment and by wishful thinking.

A ▶ 4:08 **LISTENING WARM-UP** VOCABULARY **EXPRESSIONS WITH** <u>MIND</u>
Read and listen. Then listen again and repeat.

make up one's mind

He's afraid of bees and spiders, but he can't make up his mind which are scarier.

change one's mind

She was planning to see the dentist, but it was too scary, so she changed her mind.

put (something) out of one's mind

She's terrified of flying, but she's trying to put any thought of accidents out of her mind.

be all in one's mind

He's afraid there's a monster under the bed. His mom says it's all in his mind.

be out of one's mind

Getting in the elevator would give him palpitations. But they think he's out of his mind to walk down thirty flights of stairs.

B **ACTIVATE VOCABULARY** Complete each definition with the correct form of an expression from the Vocabulary.

1 When you .... , you try not to let it worry or bother you.

2 When you .... to do something, you decide to do it no matter what happens.

3 When something is not real and a person is imagining it, you can tell the person, "............................... ."

4 When you .... , you change your opinion or decision about something.

5 If people believe you .... , they think you're behaving in a way that is crazy or foolish.

C ▶ 4:09 **LISTEN FOR DETAILS** Listen to an interview. Then complete each statement, based on the interview.

1 Many people think phobias are ...... because phobias are irrational.

   a scary   **b** funny   **c** enormous

2 People who don't suffer from phobias find them difficult to ....

   a treat   **b** overcome   **c** understand

3 Phobias create both mental and ...... symptoms.

   a economic   **b** physical   **c** irrational

4 People with phobias can't ...... them.

   a control   **b** cure   **c** confront

5 The fight-or-flight response is a set of uncomfortable physical ....

   a fears   **b** anxieties   **c** symptoms

6 Exposure therapy and counter-conditioning are two effective ....

   a treatments   **b** symptoms   **c** responses

D ▶4:10 **LISTEN TO CONFIRM CONTENT** Listen to the interview again. Write a checkmark next to the topics that were discussed in the interview and an X next to the ones that weren't. Then with a partner, summarize what was said about each topic that you checked.

☐ The number of people worldwide who suffer from phobias

☐ The way to avoid developing a phobia

☐ Some kinds of phobias that exist

☐ The danger of a rapid heartbeat

☐ The reason why people make jokes about phobias

☐ The physical responses to extreme fear

☐ Two popular treatments for phobias

E ▶4:11 **WORD STUDY** **NOUN AND ADJECTIVE FORMS** Read the noun and adjective forms that name and describe a person who suffers from acrophobia. Use the same spelling pattern to complete the chart for the other phobias. Then listen and repeat.

Phobia	Noun	Adjective
acrophobia [heights]	acrophobe	acrophobic
agoraphobia [open spaces]		
arachnophobia [spiders]		
aerophobia [flying]		
claustrophobia [enclosed spaces]		
ophidiophobia [snakes]		
xenophobia [foreigners]		

NOW YOU CAN Discuss phobias

A **NOTEPADDING** On the notepad, write some things you are afraid of. Look at the list of phobias in Word Study for ideas. Do you think your fears are just run-of-the-mill fears, or could you have real phobias?

Fear	Just afraid, or phobic?	What happens?
bees	I'm really phobic!	I get sweaty palms and palpitations. I go inside immediately!

Fear	Just afraid, or phobic?	What happens?

B **PAIR WORK** Compare notes with a partner. Ask your partner questions about his or her fears, their effects on him or her, and why he or she is frightened of the thing. Listen and offer advice.

❝ How come you're so afraid of snakes? Have you ever seen one? ❞

❝ Actually, no, I haven't. But snakes really freak me out. I think I'm just afraid, not phobic. ❞

❝ Well, maybe it would help to read about snakes to find out which are dangerous. Most are actually harmless. ❞

C **DISCUSSION** Discuss the most common fears in your class and how the fears affect your classmates in their everyday and professional lives. Provide examples.

RECYCLE THIS LANGUAGE
• ___ gives me physical symptoms. • I get butterflies in my stomach.
• My hands shake. • Don't freak out.
• I get palpitations. • Chill.
• I lose my voice. • Hang in there.
• I get sweaty palms. • I know what you mean.

83

A   WRITING SKILL   Study the rules.

When the subject and verb are separated by other words, the subject and verb must still agree.

> **Beliefs** in a supernatural event **are** common in many cultures.
> **The smart thing to do** when someone tells you something is unlucky **is** to just listen.

When two subjects are connected with <u>and</u> in a sentence, the verb must be plural.

> **A black cat** and **a broken mirror are** symbols of bad luck in several cultures.

When verbs occur in a sequence, all the verbs must agree with the subject.

> My sister **believes** in ghosts, **avoids** the number 13, and **wears** a lucky charm on a chain around her neck.

When the subject is an indefinite pronoun like <u>each</u>, <u>everyone</u>, <u>anyone</u>, <u>somebody</u>, or <u>no one</u>, use a singular verb.

> **Nobody** I know **worries** about the evil eye.

When the subject is <u>all</u>, <u>some</u>, or <u>none</u> and refers to a singular count noun or a non-count noun, use a singular verb. Otherwise use a plural verb.

> If salt is spilled by accident, **some is** immediately thrown over the shoulder.
> Some superstitions are old-fashioned, but **some are** not.

> **Remember:** Subjects and verbs must always agree in number.
> > **A superstition is** a belief many people think is irrational.
> > **Many people believe** certain things can bring good luck.

B   PRACTICE   Read the paragraph and rewrite it on a separate sheet of paper, correcting the errors in subject-verb agreement.

DIGITAL
WRITING
PROCESS

C   APPLY THE WRITING SKILL   On a separate sheet of paper, write a four-paragraph essay. In your first paragraph, introduce the topic of superstitions in general, explaining what they are and why people might believe them. Then write one paragraph each about two superstitions. Include a concluding paragraph and be sure each paragraph has a topic sentence. Be sure all your verbs and subjects agree in number.

ERROR CORRECTION

One common superstition in Western countries concern the number 13. Because they are considered unlucky, many situations involving the number 13 is frequently avoided. For example, in the past, the thirteenth floor of tall apartment buildings were often labeled "fourteen." While that is rare today, there are still many people who are uncomfortable renting an apartment on the thirteenth floor. In addition, there is a general belief that Friday the thirteenth brings bad luck, increases the chance of mishaps, and make it more difficult to get things done effectively.

SELF-CHECK

☐ Did I introduce the topic of superstitions in general in my first paragraph?

☐ Did my second and third paragraphs each describe a superstition?

☐ Did all my paragraphs include topic sentences?

☐ Did all my subjects and verbs agree?

In some cultures, black cats are considered to be unlucky.

A ▶ 4:12 **Listen to the conversations. After each conversation, summarize the claim that the people are talking about. Then listen again. After each conversation, decide whether the people find the claim believable, unlikely, or ridiculous.**

	What is the claim?	believable	unlikely	ridiculous
1		○	○	○
2		○	○	○
3		○	○	○

B Correct the errors in article usage.

A lucky charm is the object that some people carry because they think it will bring the good luck. My lucky charm is a rabbit's foot that I received as gift on my birthday. I don't really know if it has ever brought me a good luck, but I always carry it in my pocket. Since medieval times, the rabbits' feet have been said to bring a good fortune because people believed that witches were capable of turning themselves into rabbits or hares when they were being chased. Both rabbits and hares are very fast animals, so witches stood a good chance of escaping if they turned into rabbits or hares. Since then, the people have carried a rabbits' feet as a good luck charm. They believe the rabbit's foot will protect them.

C Rewrite each sentence, using a present or past passive form of the reporting verb, depending on the information in the sentence.

1 (estimate) Ten percent of people worldwide suffer from some sort of phobia.

....

2 (believe) The mind and body were completely separate, but now we know otherwise.

....

3 (say) If a bee enters your home, you will soon have a visitor.

....

4 (claim) If you say good-bye to a friend on a bridge, you'll never see that friend again.

....

5 (think) The house was damaged by lightning before the fire, but that turned out not to be true.

....

D Choose the correct expression to complete each sentence.

1 If you have a fear of spiders, you should ...... that spiders are very easy to kill.

   a make up your mind   **b** keep in mind

2 Though he was hesitant at first, in the end he ...... to seek help for his problem.

   a was out of his mind   **b** made up his mind

3 She made the decision to get married, but a month before the wedding, she ....

   a changed her mind   **b** kept it in mind

4 People who have a phobia find it very difficult to ....

   a make up their mind   **b** put it out of their mind

TEST-TAKING SKILLS BOOSTER p. 157

Web Project: Phobias
www.english.com/summit3e

UNIT

8

Performing at Your Best

COMMUNICATION GOALS

1 Discuss your talents and strengths
2 Suggest ways to boost intelligence
3 Explain how you produce your best work
4 Describe what makes someone a "genius"

PREVIEW

A FRAME YOUR IDEAS Take the EQ quiz.

HOW EMOTIONALLY
INTELLIGENT ARE YOU?

The concept of emotional intelligence, developed by psychologist Daniel Goleman, is described as the ability to understand one's own emotions and those of others and use them to motivate actions and achieve goals. According to Goleman, one's emotional intelligence quotient (EQ) can be high even if one's standard intelligence test score (IQ) is low. Take the quiz to calculate your EQ. Check each statement that is true for you. Be as honest as you can!

○ When I feel down, I try to focus on positive things.

○ I like learning about new things.

○ I'm not the kind of person who overreacts to things.

○ I find it easy to admit when I've made a mistake.

○ I see mistakes as opportunities to learn.

○ Most people agree that I have a good sense of humor.

○ When I'm upset about something, I usually know exactly what's bothering me.

○ Understanding the way other people feel or think is important to me.

○ When people criticize me, I use it as an opportunity to improve myself.

○ I don't mind talking with others about uncomfortable topics.

○ I find it fairly easy to get along with people I don't like.

○ I have a good awareness of how my own behavior affects others.

○ I don't mind conflicts or disagreements.

○ I'm good at helping people who disagree with each other to reach a solution.

○ It's easy to motivate myself to do things I don't really want to do.

○ Before making an important decision, I usually ask other people for advice.

○ I always think about the ethical consequences of the decisions I make.

○ I have a clear idea of what my strengths and weaknesses are.

○ I feel satisfied with my accomplishments, even if I haven't received any praise.

○ I generally feel good about who I am, even though there may be things I'd like to change.

SCORE How many statements did you check?

17–20 = you have a very high EQ   **5–8** = you have a below-average EQ
13–16 = you have an above-average EQ   **1–4** = you have a very low EQ
9–12 = you have an average EQ

B PAIR WORK Compare scores with a partner. Do you each feel that your score accurately measures your emotional intelligence? Explain.

C DISCUSSION According to Goleman, emotional intelligence is more important for an employee's success than either technical skills or IQ. Based on the quiz, in what ways does EQ seem to measure intelligence differently from IQ? Why might an EQ score be useful for an employer to know?

D ▶ 4:13 **SPOTLIGHT**   Read and listen to a conversation in which someone expresses concern about a family member. Notice the spotlighted language.

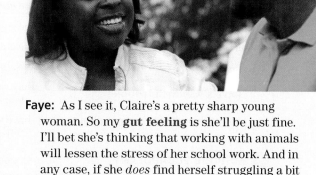

Faye: Tony, how's your youngest daughter doing?

Tony: Claire? Here's the thing … She's just a year away from finishing her engineering degree. And, **out of the blue**, she decides to take a part-time job at an animal shelter, taking care of cats!

Faye: Well, that's not surprising. Claire's very responsible. And she's always had a way with animals. I assume she's doing it to help pay for college?

Tony: That's what she said. But in my view she really needs to **put her nose to the grindstone** and focus on her studies right now. Engineering is a tough subject.

Faye: So you're worried it'll affect her grades?

Tony: Exactly. This is her final year. **It's now or never**.

Faye: Have you tried talking with her? Maybe she'll see your point and reconsider.

Tony: Are you kidding? With Claire, everything I say **goes in one ear and out the other**.

Faye: Well, if you don't mind, I'll tell you what I think. Can I be frank?

Tony: Please.

Faye: As I see it, Claire's a pretty sharp young woman. So my **gut feeling** is she'll be just fine. I'll bet she's thinking that working with animals will lessen the stress of her school work. And in any case, if she *does* find herself struggling a bit in her studies, she could always quit the job and concentrate on catching up. I think you should stop worrying about her.

Tony: **I can't help it** … She's my baby girl. But you're probably right. Of my three kids, she's the one I least need to worry about. She's always been very focused on achieving her goals.

E **UNDERSTAND IDIOMS AND EXPRESSIONS**   Match the statement parts to define the idioms and expressions from Spotlight.

1 When you do something "out of the blue," ..... .

2 When you "put your nose to the grindstone," ..... .

3 When you say "It's now or never," ..... .

4 When something "goes in one ear and out the other," ..... .

5 When you have a "gut feeling," ..... .

6 When you say "I can't help it," ..... .

a it's the last opportunity to do something

b you're unable to stop doing something

c someone isn't listening

d you do it suddenly without warning

e you have a strong sense about something

f you're working hard

F **PERSONALIZE IDIOMS AND EXPRESSIONS**
Use two or more idioms from Ex. E to tell a partner about a time when you were concerned about someone or gave someone advice.

❝ My sister wasn't sure what to study, but I had a gut feeling she would like mathematics. So I recommended that she take a course. Unfortunately, my advice went in one ear and out the other … ❞

SPEAKING   Use the EQ quiz to analyze the emotional intelligence of the three characters in Spotlight: Tony, Claire, and Faye. Explain your thinking.

❝ Claire doesn't seem to want to listen to her father's advice. However, according to the quiz, a part of being emotionally intelligent is asking for other people's advice before making important decisions. ❞

❝ I think Faye's a good listener. She seems pretty good at helping people who disagree with each other to reach a solution. ❞

GOAL Discuss your talents and strengths

A ▶ 4:14 **VOCABULARY** EXPRESSIONS TO DESCRIBE TALENTS AND STRENGTHS
DIGITAL STRATEGIES

Read and listen. Then listen again and repeat.

be good with one's hands	have the ability to use one's hands to make or do things
be mechanically inclined	be able to understand how machines work
have a head for figures	be good at mathematical calculations
have an ear for music	be good at recognizing, remembering, and imitating musical sounds
have an eye for detail	be good at seeing or paying attention to things that others don't usually notice
have a good intuitive sense	be able to draw conclusions based on feelings rather than facts
have a way with words	be able to express one's ideas and opinions well
have a way with [people]	have a special ability to work well with someone or something, for example, plants, children, or animals
have a knack for [learning languages]	have a natural skill or ability to do something well

B **ACTIVATE VOCABULARY** With a partner, use the expressions in the Vocabulary to describe each person's talents and strengths. There may be more than one way to do so. Explain your reasons.

❝ Clearly Adela has a knack for learning languages! ❞

Adela Petran can speak nine languages, including her native Romanian. "It's really not difficult at all," she says.

Miguel Asturias began writing poetry when he was 12. Even though he is still a teen, his teachers have encouraged him to enter his poems in competitions.

Kim Jin-ho was able to solve university math problems at the age of ten. He now teaches math. He argues, "Math's only hard if you think it's going to be hard."

Aiko Kato began playing the violin at the age of three. Today she plays with the Nagoya Philharmonic Orchestra.

Leilah Zaman has been successful at making and selling her own line of women's clothing for five years now. She does all the sewing herself.

As a kid, **Felipe Morais** liked to take electronic devices apart to figure out how they worked. By the age of 16, he knew he wanted to study engineering.

Blair O'Connor works as an editor. Her job is to check manuscripts for errors and correct them before they get published.

Salesman **Bob Pryor** is a good listener. He pays attention to his customers' needs and can anticipate what they want before they even know it.

C **PERSONALIZE** Use the Vocabulary to describe five or six people you know.

❝ My brother Gene, who is a family doctor, has a really good intuitive sense. He can tell what's bothering his patients even when they can't. ❞

DIGITAL INDUCTIVE ACTIVITY
D **GRAMMAR** USING AUXILIARY <u>DO</u> FOR EMPHATIC STRESS

To add emphatic stress to an affirmative statement in the simple present or past tense, use <u>do</u> or <u>did</u> before the base form of the verb.

Even if I don't have a head for figures, I **do** have a way with words.
He **did** like most of his colleagues, but he didn't like his boss.

Be careful!
Use a base form after a form of the auxiliary <u>do</u>.

She has an eye for detail. → She **does have** an eye for detail. NOT She ~~does has~~ ...
He liked his job. → He **did like** his job. NOT He ~~did liked~~ ...

▶ 4:15 **Listen to emphatic stress on the auxiliary <u>do</u>. Then listen and repeat.**
I do have an ear for music.
She does have an ear for music.
He did like his colleagues.

GRAMMAR BOOSTER p. 140
Emphatic stress

E GRAMMAR PRACTICE On a separate sheet of paper, rewrite each item, using <u>do</u> or <u>did</u> for emphatic stress.

1 Sam isn't a great cook. However, he <u>makes</u> great desserts.

2 You're absolutely right! I <u>put things off</u> way too often.

3 She may not sing very well, but she <u>knows</u> how to dance.

4 We made total fools of ourselves, but we <u>got</u> everyone to laugh.

5 He's never lived abroad, but he <u>has</u> a knack for languages.

6 Her decision to quit her job really <u>happened</u> out of the blue.

> *Sam isn't a great cook. However, he does make great desserts.*

PRONUNCIATION BOOSTER p. 148

Emphatic stress with auxiliary verbs

F PAIR WORK On a separate sheet of paper, write five statements comparing your talents and strengths with your weaknesses, using the auxiliary <u>do</u> for emphatic stress. With a partner, take turns reading your statements aloud.

> 66 I don't have an eye for detail, but I *do* have a strong intuitive sense. 99

NOW YOU CAN Discuss your talents and strengths

A ▶4:16 CONVERSATION SPOTLIGHT Read and listen. Notice the spotlighted conversation strategies.

A: **Guess what**? I've decided to sign up for an online course.

B: Fantastic! What are you going to be studying?

A: I'm not sure yet. **I can't make up my mind between** engineering and psychology.

B: Which subject do you think you have the most talent for?

A: Well, **I wouldn't say** I'm mechanically inclined, but I do have lots of ability in math.

B: Then maybe engineering would be a good fit.

A: Maybe. But **I've also been told that** I have a good intuitive sense.

B: **I don't think you can go wrong**. Either choice sounds great. Besides, you could always switch subjects down the road if you want.

B ▶4:17 RHYTHM AND INTONATION Listen again and repeat. Then practice the conversation with a partner.

C CONVERSATION ACTIVATOR Role-play a similar conversation in which you discuss your talents and strengths. Use the Vocabulary and emphatic stress with the auxiliary <u>do</u>. Start like this: *Guess what?* Be sure to change roles and then partners. OPTION: Tell your classmates about your partner's talents and strengths.

DON'T STOP!

- Provide more details about your talents and strengths.
- Provide more details about what you would like to be able to do.
- Talk about the talents and strengths of people you know.
- Say as much as you can.

RECYCLE THIS LANGUAGE

- I'm [good at / not so good at] ___ .
- I wish I [were / weren't] ___ .
- I wish I [had / hadn't] ___ .
- If only I [could / would] ___ .
- My gut feeling is ___ .
- It's now or never.

GOAL Suggest ways to boost intelligence

A ▶ 4:18 **GRAMMAR SPOTLIGHT**   Read the article and notice the spotlighted grammar.

CAN INTELLIGENCE BE INCREASED?

In a general sense, intelligence can be defined as the ability to learn, understand, and apply knowledge or skills. In order to maximize these abilities, many argue that it's essential **that the brain not be allowed** to get lazy. Anything from reading more to doing puzzles regularly to learning a new language may in fact improve our thinking skills, capacity to remember, and general knowledge.

IQ (intelligence quotient) has long been used as a measure of intelligence based on general knowledge, mathematical and verbal ability, logic, and memory. While many experts insist **that IQ test scores not be seen** as changeable, others have pointed out that IQ tests provide an incomplete and inadequate measure of real intelligence. To some degree, they measure how one's level of academic achievement can be predicted, but do not measure creativity or "street smarts"—the ability to cope with everyday life. And they do not measure one's potential for growth.

Some experts suggest **that other aspects of intelligence be considered** as well—emotional intelligence being one example. Harvard University's Howard Gardner proposed **that psychologists and educators recognize** the following distinct areas of intelligence: *linguistic* and *mathematical* (which are currently measured to some degree by IQ tests), *interpersonal*—how successfully we interact with others—and *intrapersonal*—how we understand ourselves (both of which are measured by EQ tests). He also proposed measuring *visual-spatial* intelligence—the ability to use and understand visual information in charts, diagrams, and art. And finally Gardner recommended **that two other aspects of intelligence be included**: *musical* (the ability to make sense of sounds) and *physical* (the intelligence that dancers and athletes show through movement). Gardner considers each of these intelligences to be areas of human potential—in other words, they can be developed and increased.

B **DISCUSSION**   Describe people you know who exhibit some of the types of intelligence proposed by Gardner.

 C **GRAMMAR**   THE SUBJUNCTIVE

Use the subjunctive form of a verb in a noun clause that follows a verb or adjective of urgency, obligation, or advisability. The subjunctive form of the verb is the same as the base form and doesn't change, no matter what the subject of the clause is. Use <u>not</u> before the verb for the negative.

> She insisted (that) we **be** at the office at three o'clock.
> I'm proposing (that) you **not apply** for that job until you've passed your driving test.
> It's important (that) he **complete** the presentation in less than thirty minutes.

The passive form of the subjunctive is <u>be</u> + the past participle.

> They suggested that my mother **not be given** an EQ test.

The continuous form of the subjunctive is <u>be</u> + the present participle.

> It's crucial that they **be waiting** outside the room after the interview.

Urgency, obligation, and advisability	
Verbs	**Adjectives**
demand	critical
insist	crucial
propose	desirable
recommend	essential
request	important
suggest	necessary
urge	

DIGITAL INDUCTIVE ACTIVITY

Note: The subjunctive in the noun clause doesn't change, no matter what the time frame of the entire sentence is.

It was essential (that) the theory **explain** (NOT ~~explained~~) how intelligence would be boosted.

The psychologist recommended (that) all her patients **be given** (NOT ~~were given~~) a standardized test of intelligence.

I will request (that) people **not be admitted** (NOT ~~will not be admitted~~) to the lecture unless they are already enrolled in the course.

They had insisted that no one **be texting** (NOT ~~were texting~~) during the meeting.

Be careful!
If a noun clause doesn't follow a verb or adjective of urgency, obligation, or advisability, don't use the subjunctive.

Scientists agree that EQ testing **is** a useful tool.

It is interesting that Gardner **identified** other kinds of intelligence.

GRAMMAR BOOSTER p. 141
Infinitives and gerunds in place of the subjunctive

D **GRAMMAR PRACTICE** Decide whether to use the subjunctive and circle the correct form. Explain each answer.

1 Jack and Shira were convinced that their daughter Sue (was / be) a genius.

2 It would be critical that every potential employee (take / took) an EQ test.

3 Everyone knows that intuitive intelligence (isn't / not be) learned in school.

4 It was important that Shelly (become / becomes) more aware of her colleague's emotions.

5 Martin demanded that the new assistant (be / was) trained to deal with customers more effectively.

6 It's crucial that she (doesn't accept / not accept) her employer's opinion about her test scores.

7 I had hoped that he (would be / be) offered the job based on his talents and abilities.

8 Jake proposed that he (didn't continue / not continue) searching for the website until after lunch.

9 Our manager insisted that no one (is / be) late for the conference call.

10 It's essential that you (be sitting / are sitting) in front of your computer at 3:00.

11 It's important that Bryce (improve / improves) his interpersonal intelligence.

> *You only use the subjunctive if the noun clause comes after a verb or adjective of urgency, obligation, or advisability.*

E **PAIR WORK** With a partner, take turns completing these statements in your own way, using the subjunctive.

1 On the first day of class, it's important that a teacher …

2 I suggest that a visitor to our city …

3 I would recommend that the government …

4 I think it's crucial that every parent …

5 When I take a taxi, I insist that the driver …

If you don't have a head for figures, it's essential that you get lots of practice.

NOW YOU CAN Suggest ways to boost intelligence

A **NOTEPADDING** Choose one or more of the intelligences mentioned in Grammar Spotlight. On your notepad, list suggestions for exercising the brain and boosting those intelligences.

Your suggestions
mathematical intelligence: do math puzzles, keep track of your personal finances

Your suggestions

Some ideas
- take a class
- play digital games
- eat brain-healthy foods
- get lots of sleep
- listen to audio lectures
- your own idea: ___

B **DISCUSSION ACTIVATOR** In a small group, share the ideas from your notes. Suggest and discuss ways to boost intelligence. Use the subjunctive in noun clauses after verbs or adjectives of urgency, obligation, or advisability. Say as much as you can.

> *I suggest you do math puzzles regularly to exercise your brain. It's important, though, that they be fun. Otherwise, you won't keep doing them.*

LESSON 3

GOAL Explain how you produce your best work

A **READING WARM-UP** Why do you think people often have problems staying on task when they have to do something? When does that happen to *you*?

DIGITAL STRATEGIES **B** ▶ 4:19 **READING** Read the article. What do you think the title "Stay on Target" means?

STAY ON TARGET

You've got work to do, but you just can't seem to get your brain going. You stare at that blank piece of paper in front of you but can't get your thoughts organized. Your mind wanders to the argument you had with your spouse, the leftovers in the fridge … Then, just as your ideas finally start to come together, the phone rings, and you're back to square one. Sound familiar? The ability to devote all of one's attention to a single task is the key to achievement in any occupation. On the other hand, being unable to concentrate can keep you from producing your best work. The following tips can help you stay focused:

Stay organized. Let's face it—it's not easy to keep focused if your desk looks like it just got hit by a tornado. Efficiency coach Selma Wilson suggests you spend a few moments a day cleaning up your workspace and reducing the time you normally spend searching for mislaid memos or your flash drive.

Develop a routine. Studies show that following a systematic pattern of behavior can make it easier to devote your undivided attention to a task. For example, if you're a student and you have trouble preparing for exams, it's critical that you establish a study ritual. Start and finish at the same time each day. Work at the same desk or in your favorite chair. If music helps you focus, choose a piece of music and play it during every study session.

Make a list. Each morning, write down all the tasks you need to accomplish that day and cross off each item as you complete it. This visual reminder will not only keep you focused on your goals but will also give you a sense of progress and achievement.

Challenge yourself. When faced with a boring, routine task that seems to drag on forever, it's easy to lose concentration and make careless mistakes. According to writer Mihaly Csikszentmihalyi, one of the best ways to engage your attention on a dull task is to make it harder. For example, turn the task into a game by giving yourself a time limit. The increased challenge stimulates blood flow and activity in the brain, making it easier for you to focus on the job at hand.

Reserve some "do not disturb" time. If interruptions from family, friends, or co-workers prevent you from getting your work done, set aside a certain period of your schedule each day when you are unavailable. Let others know that they shouldn't disturb you during this time. Close the door to your office or find an area where you're less likely to be interrupted by colleagues, such as a conference room or a quiet coffee shop with Wi-Fi.

Go offline. While the Internet is an invaluable tool for getting and sharing information, it can be a real concentration killer. If all those quick clicks to "just check the news" are interfering with your productivity, Wilson recommends you make it a point to stay offline while you're working. And if you find your focus constantly broken by incoming e-mail and instant messages, do resist the urge to read and reply to them as they arrive. Instead, set aside certain times of the day for your e-mail—and keep working.

Take a breather. Taking short breaks can help you clear your mind and refocus on the next job. Stand up for a moment and take a short walk in the hallway or just close your eyes, relax your muscles, and breathe deeply.

The next time you have an important project that requires your full concentration, see if any of these strategies can make a difference for you.

APPLY IDEAS Which tip from the article has each person applied? Explain your choices.

KYOKO is having trouble getting started writing an article about a topic that doesn't inspire her. When a colleague suggests she begin every paragraph with the letter S, the words start flowing smoothly.

TATANIA has to study for two important university exams tomorrow. She studies intensely but takes regular fifteen-minute breaks to relax. Before starting to study for the second exam, she takes a long walk in the park.

EMILIO is a classical singer. At every concert, just before going on stage, he always does the same thing. He slowly drinks half a cup of tea with honey and he texts his daughter just to say hello. Then he feels ready to go on.

CLAUDIO has decided to decrease distractions by setting up a separate e-mail account for his friends and family so they don't mix with his office e-mails. He makes it a strict rule to check the account for messages only during lunch or after hours.

MARINA has two young teens and works at home. From 12:00 to 3:00 each day, she keeps the door to her home office closed and turns her smartphone off. Her kids know that it's crucial that they not knock on the door or call her unless it's an emergency.

JAE JIN is responsible for five major projects, and by the end of the day, his work area is always a mess, covered with memos and files. Before leaving the office each day, he makes a point of taking five minutes to organize all the papers on his desk.

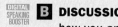 **D** **RELATE TO PERSONAL EXPERIENCE** With a partner, discuss which of the tips in the article seem the most useful and explain your reasons. If you have ever tried any of them, describe the results.

NOW YOU CAN Explain how you produce your best work

A **NOTEPADDING** On your notepad, list the distractions that cause you to lose focus when you are working on a task. What strategies do you use to stay focused?

I lose focus when …	I stay focused by …
I'm interrupted by phone calls.	not answering calls.

I lose focus when …	I stay focused by …

Some distractions
• noise
• phone calls
• interruptions
• worries
• aches and pains
• room temperature
• hunger
• boredom

B **DISCUSSION** What conditions help you produce your best work? Compare how you and your classmates stay focused and how you overcome distractions.

"I work best when it's very quiet. If I'm reading, I can't concentrate when I get interrupted. So I just close the door to let people know they shouldn't disturb me."

GOAL Describe what makes someone a "genius"

A **LISTENING WARM-UP DISCUSSION** In your opinion, is there a difference between describing someone as intelligent and calling him or her a genius? Explain.

B ▶ 4:20 **LISTEN FOR MAIN IDEAS** Listen to Part 1 of a lecture on human intelligence. Choose the speaker's main point.

1 Everyone with a high IQ is a genius.

2 Not everyone agrees about how to define genius.

3 A genius is someone with an IQ score over 145.

C ▶ 4:21 **LISTEN TO INFER** Listen to Part 1 again and pay attention to the opposing arguments. Check the one statement that best supports the argument that a high IQ score doesn't determine whether one is a genius.

Albert Einstein, physicist and Nobel Prize winner

☐ Albert Einstein had an IQ of 160 and had many impressive achievements.

☐ Most average people have an IQ score that can range from about 85 to 115.

☐ Most people agree that the composer Beethoven was probably a genius.

☐ The 1,500 gifted children in Terman's study had IQs of 140 or more.

☐ None of the people with high IQs in Terman's research had any notable achievements.

D ▶ 4:22 **LISTEN FOR SUPPORTING DETAILS** Now listen to Part 2 of the lecture. Write at least two arguments the lecturer mentions to support each theory.

Srinivasa Ramanujan, mathematician

in favor of a genetic theory	in favor of an environmental theory
1	1
2	2

E ▶ 4:23 **VOCABULARY** ADJECTIVES THAT DESCRIBE ASPECTS OF INTELLIGENCE Read and listen. Then listen again and repeat.

talented	having a natural ability to do something very well
perceptive / observant	good at noticing what people are thinking or feeling
inventive / imaginative	good at thinking of new and interesting ideas; creative
witty	able to use humor intelligently; good at using words for others' enjoyment
curious / inquisitive	having the desire to learn about new things
open-minded	willing to consider new ideas; not close-minded
persistent	willing to continue trying something in spite of difficulty

F **VOCABULARY PRACTICE** Choose the best adjective to complete each description.

1 Comedian Helen Hong's success can be attributed to her (persistent / perceptive) and very funny observations of everyday life.

2 Colombian novelist Gabriel García Márquez was one of the world's most (inventive / inquisitive) writers. He was famous for creating fantastic stories and images.

3 Mark Twain, whose real name was Samuel Clemens, was a (persistent / witty) writer and storyteller. His accounts of his world travels still make people laugh.

4 Jane Goodall is known for her ground-breaking work studying chimpanzees. Her (inquisitive / inventive) mind helped her consider questions about chimp behavior that had never been explained before.

5 Korean film director Bong Joon-ho has been praised as one of the most (talented / persistent) artists in recent years for his excellent imaginative movies.

G **PERSONALIZE THE VOCABULARY** With a partner, use each adjective to describe a person you know or have heard or read about.

> ❝I'd call my nephew Sam very imaginative. He's only eight years old, but he entertains us with fantastic stories all the time. ❞

> ❝I think the Chinese pianist Yuja Wang is really talented. Her interpretations of pieces by classical composers are very perceptive. I always feel like I'm hearing something new when she plays. ❞

NOW YOU CAN   Describe what makes someone a "genius"

A **NOTEPADDING** Identify someone—famous or not—who you would consider to be extremely intelligent or even a genius. In what ways would you describe aspects of this person's intelligence? Write notes about the person on your notepad. Use the Vocabulary from this lesson and from page 88.

> Who is it? *my uncle Morris*
>
> List his or her abilities and traits of intelligence:
>
> - really sharp, has an incredible head for figures and a way with words
>
> - a little eccentric, extremely perceptive

Who is it?

List his or her abilities and traits of intelligence:

Do you think this person's intelligence came from the environment or his or her genes? Why?

Would you call this person a genius? Why or why not?

B **DISCUSSION** With a partner, discuss the person you wrote about on your notepad. Explain where, in your opinion, the person got his or her intelligence from, providing examples from the person's background and environment.

RECYCLE THIS LANGUAGE		
· difficult	· energetic	· outgoing
· easygoing	· gifted	· passionate
· eccentric	· hardworking	· serious
· egotistical	· moody	· sharp

OPTIONAL WRITING Write about the person you discussed. Support your view that this person has above-average intelligence with examples.

A WRITING SKILL   Study the rules.

In formal writing, connecting words and phrases are commonly used to clarify relationships between ideas. Use the following to focus on causes or results.

Causes

Use one of these phrases to focus on a cause.

Due to __ ,	Because of __ ,
As a result of __ ,	As a consequence of __ ,

┌─────── cause ───────┐
As a result of a high workload, our work area may get messy.

                              ┌─────────── cause ───────────┐
It may be difficult to stay on task **due to constant interruptions by colleagues.**

Results

Begin a sentence with one of these words or phrases to focus on a result.

As a result,	Consequently,
As a consequence,	Therefore,

                              ┌─────────── result ───────────┐
Colleagues may constantly interrupt your work. **Consequently,** it may be difficult to stay focused.

B PRACTICE   In the Writing Model, underline five sentences with connecting words or phrases that clarify causes and results. Then, on a separate sheet of paper, rewrite each sentence twice, using a different connecting word or phrase.

C APPLY THE WRITING SKILL   Write a three-paragraph essay about the challenges of staying focused while trying to complete a task. Use the "outline" below as a guide. Be sure to include connecting words and phrases to signal causes and results.

Paragraph 1
Describe the things that make staying focused difficult. Summarize the causes.

Paragraph 2
Describe the results of not being able to stay focused.

Paragraph 3
Suggest some ways one might overcome the challenges and become more focused on completing a task.

WRITING MODEL

When trying to focus on a task, you may discover there are numerous distractions that can keep you from completing your work. You may find it difficult to stay focused due to your staying up late the night before. As a consequence of frequent interruptions by colleagues, you may feel like you are always starting the task all over again. Anything can distract you from a task, and the results can be harmful.

Not being able to stay focused can affect your work in negative ways. You may not be able to produce a report for your manager by the time he or she expects it. Consequently, your manager may wonder whether or not he or she can count on you to deliver what you have promised. Your colleagues may depend on you to finish a task, but you are unable to do it. As a result, you risk your reputation at work.

If you are having difficulty completing a task, it is important that you take actions that help you stay on target. Because of frequent interruptions, you may have to close your office door or ask your colleagues not to disturb you. If you are suffering from a lack of sleep, you may have to take a break and grab a cup of coffee before you start. As long as you make an effort, you should be able to get back on target.

SELF-CHECK

☐ Did my paragraphs follow the content and sequence suggested in Exercise C?

☐ Did I use connecting phrases to focus on causes?

☐ Did I introduce sentences with connecting words or phrases to focus on results?

A ▶ 4:24 Listen to a teacher talking to parents about their children. After each conversation, check the statement that best describes each child's talents and abilities. Listen again if necessary.

1 Liza
- [ ] has a head for figures.
- [ ] has a way with words.
- [ ] has a knack for languages.

2 Ben
- [ ] is mechanically inclined.
- [ ] has a good intuitive sense.
- [ ] is good with his hands.

3 Stella
- [ ] has a knack for languages.
- [ ] has an ear for music.
- [ ] has a way with words.

4 Steven
- [ ] has a good intuitive sense.
- [ ] has a way with people.
- [ ] has a head for figures.

5 Sophie
- [ ] has an ear for music.
- [ ] has a way with words.
- [ ] has a knack for languages.

6 Dan
- [ ] has an eye for detail.
- [ ] has a good intuitive sense.
- [ ] is mechanically inclined.

7 Karen
- [ ] has a way with words.
- [ ] has an eye for detail.
- [ ] is good with her hands.

8 Sam
- [ ] has a head for figures.
- [ ] has a good intuitive sense.
- [ ] has a way with people.

B Find and correct the six errors in using the subjunctive.

Dr. Howard Gardner believes that genius is determined by the environment. Therefore, he recommends that children are provided with greater educational opportunities in order to develop their talents. Other psychologists, however, think that genius is inherited. According to them, if a child is born with talent, it is crucial that he or she receives special attention.

According to Dr. Gardner, people have different kinds of intelligence, and there are different ways of learning suitable for each intelligence type. Consequently, he proposes that a teacher uses learning strategies that are best suited to a particular student's type of intelligence. For example, Gardner suggests that a student studies alone if he or she has intrapersonal intelligence. If, on the other hand, the learner has interpersonal intelligence, it is important that the student works in a team.

Because characteristics such as motivation and emotional control are considered important in the workplace, more and more employers insist that a job applicant takes an EQ test to help the manager make hiring decisions.

C Write the correct letter to complete each definition.

1 A person who is witty ....
2 A person who is inquisitive ....
3 A person who is inventive ....
4 A person who is very perceptive ....
5 A person who is really sharp ....
6 A person who is open-minded ....
7 A person who is persistent ....

a keeps trying, even when things are tough
b is probably comfortable with people who disagree with his or her opinions
c is comfortable relying on gut feelings to make decisions
d enjoys learning about new things
e entertains friends with funny and intelligent stories
f has a talent for creating new ideas
g is smart and quick at figuring things out

TEST-TAKING SKILLS BOOSTER p. 158

Web Project: Emotional Intelligence
www.english.com/summit3e

UNIT 9

What Lies Ahead?

COMMUNICATION GOALS

1 Discuss the feasibility of future technologies
2 Evaluate applications of innovative technologies
3 Discuss how to protect our future environment
4 Examine future social and demographic trends

PREVIEW

A FRAME YOUR IDEAS Complete the survey.

WILL IT COME TRUE?

Which of the following predictions do you think will come true by the end of the 21st century? Which are just too wild to come true? Check your responses on a scale of probability from unlikely to definitely. Add your own predictions if you have any.

MEDICINE AND HEALTH

1 The majority of surgeries will be performed by robots.

UNLIKELY   POSSIBLY   LIKELY   DEFINITELY

2 Scientists will have discovered effective cures for cancer and heart disease.

UNLIKELY   POSSIBLY   LIKELY   DEFINITELY

3 Eyeglasses will have become obsolete.

UNLIKELY   POSSIBLY   LIKELY   DEFINITELY

4 Most people will live to be over 100 years old.

UNLIKELY   POSSIBLY   LIKELY   DEFINITELY

5 Your prediction:

_____

TRANSPORTATION

1 Petroleum will no longer be used as an energy source.

UNLIKELY   POSSIBLY   LIKELY   DEFINITELY

2 Most vehicles will not require a driver.

UNLIKELY   POSSIBLY   LIKELY   DEFINITELY

3 Commercial space travel will be available to anyone who can afford it.

UNLIKELY   POSSIBLY   LIKELY   DEFINITELY

4 Digital technology will have replaced the traditional paper passport.

UNLIKELY   POSSIBLY   LIKELY   DEFINITELY

5 Your prediction:

_____

_____

HOME AND WORK

1 People will be living on another planet.

UNLIKELY   POSSIBLY   LIKELY   DEFINITELY

2 Agricultural work will no longer require human workers.

UNLIKELY   POSSIBLY   LIKELY   DEFINITELY

3 The majority of homes will have a robot to do household chores.

UNLIKELY   POSSIBLY   LIKELY   DEFINITELY

4 Most people will work and make a living from their own homes.

UNLIKELY   POSSIBLY   LIKELY   DEFINITELY

5 Your prediction:

_____

_____

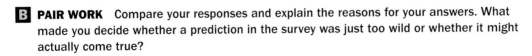

B PAIR WORK Compare your responses and explain the reasons for your answers. What made you decide whether a prediction in the survey was just too wild or whether it might actually come true?

C ▶ 5:02 **SPOTLIGHT**   Read and listen to a conversation about the uses for a new technology. Notice the spotlighted language.

Lena: I just read that packages are going to be delivered to people's homes using drones. Is that cool or what?

Nate: Well, it's shocking how much they seem to **be catching on**. You never know where you're going to see them next.

Lena: That's true.

Nate: Unfortunately, no matter how you look at it, it's just going to **open a can of worms**.

Lena: Really? In what way?

Nate: I just think the more drones, the more unintended consequences.

Lena: Sorry. I don't get it. Drones seem pretty harmless to me.

Nate: Well, think about it. Imagine thousands of drones flying all over the place. Who's going to make sure they don't crash into each other? **Before you know it**, somebody's going to get hurt.

Lena: **Come to think of it**, I read last week that some have already crashed into cars … and even people!

Nate: And from what I understand, that**'s just scratching the surface**. It gets worse. Pilots have been reporting sightings of drones during takeoffs and landings.

Lena: Wow! That's no joke!

Nate: Exactly. At some point there's going to be a collision—**it isn't a question of if but when**.

Lena: Well, this is definitely a case in which **the bad outweighs the good**.

D **UNDERSTAND IDIOMS AND EXPRESSIONS**   Find these idioms and expressions in Spotlight. Complete each explanation by writing the correct letter.

.... **1** Say something "is catching on" to …

.... **2** Say "It'll open a can of worms" to …

.... **3** Say "Before you know it" to …

.... **4** Say "Come to think of it" to …

.... **5** Say "It's just scratching the surface" to …

.... **6** Say "It isn't a question of if but when" to …

.... **7** Say "The bad outweighs the good" to …

a indicate you suddenly realize or remember something.

b suggest that it provides only a small piece of the total picture.

c suggest that something is going to happen soon.

d suggest that there are more disadvantages than advantages.

e indicate that something is becoming popular.

f state that something is certain to happen.

g express concern about possible problems in the future.

E **DISCUSSION**

1 What are some current uses for drones you're familiar with? What are some possible uses in the future? Use your own ideas.

2 Summarize Nate's concerns about the consequences of an increased use of drone technology. Do you agree with his concerns, or do you think drones are harmless? Explain your views.

SPEAKING   Which of the predictions from page 98 do you think would open a can of worms? Use expressions from Spotlight. Explain your reasons.

❝I'd worry that digital passports might open a can of worms. Before you know it, criminals or terrorists would be stealing people's identities. ❞

❝If robots do household chores, people will get lazy! Let's face it … the bad outweighs the good. ❞

GOAL Discuss the feasibility of future technologies

A ▶5:03 **GRAMMAR SPOTLIGHT** Read the article and notice the spotlighted grammar.

ENVISIONING THE **FUTURE**

In the 1960s, only large institutions, such as banks, corporations, and the military, had computers. They were expensive, slow, and very large—requiring a special air-conditioned room—and access to them was limited to only a few people. In the 1970s, computer prices came down and then small businesses began to use them. Nevertheless, in 1977, the CEO and founder of Digital Equipment, Kenneth Olsen, predicted that computers **would never be used** in the home.

> Computers **are never going to be used** in the home.

Kenneth Olsen

In the early 1980s, Steve Jobs and Bill Gates introduced the personal computer—the Macintosh and the IBM PC, respectively—which made computing at home possible. In 1983, Jobs gave a speech about the future, in which he predicted that, for most people, a great deal of time **would be spent** interacting with personal computers. He also predicted that, within ten years, computers in the office and at home **would be connected** so people would be able to use them to communicate.

> In the future, a great amount of our time **is going to be spent** interacting with our personal computers. And in ten years, home and office computers **will have been connected** to each other so people can use them to communicate and keep in touch.

Steve Jobs

In 1999, Gates predicted that small devices **would be carried** around by everyone so that they could get instant information and stay in touch with others. He also claimed that, by the early 21st century, Internet communities **would have been formed**, based on one's interests or to connect with friends and family.

> Small devices **will be carried** around by everyone to get information and stay in touch. And in the early 21st century, Internet communities **will have been formed**.

Bill Gates

B **DISCUSSION** Which of the twentieth century predictions about computers have come true? In what ways?

PRONUNCIATION BOOSTER	p. 149

Reading aloud

DIGITAL INDUCTIVE ACTIVITY

C **GRAMMAR** THE PASSIVE VOICE: THE FUTURE, THE FUTURE AS SEEN FROM THE PAST, AND THE FUTURE PERFECT

Passive voice statements about the future: <u>will be</u> (or <u>be going to be</u>) + a past participle

> In the future, appliances **will be linked** to each other and to the Internet as well.
> In coming years, our lives **are going to be made** easier by new home technologies.

Passive voice statements about the future as seen from the past: <u>would be</u> (or <u>was / were going to be</u>) + a past participle

> Jobs and Gates predicted that computers **would be used** by millions of people at home.
> Olsen thought that computers **were** never **going to be purchased** for use at home.

Passive voice statements in the future perfect: <u>will have been</u> (or <u>be going to have been</u>) + a past participle

> By 2050, commercial airplanes **will have been redesigned** to be much quieter.
> In a few decades, the TV set **is going to have been made** obsolete.

Note: The passive voice is often used when discussing science and technology.

Use a <u>by</u> phrase when it's important to name the agent (the performer of the action).

> Our lives will be improved **by technology**.

GRAMMAR BOOSTER	p. 141

When to use the passive voice

D GRAMMAR PRACTICE Look at the predictions for a possible moon habitat. On a separate sheet of paper, change the statements from active to passive voice.

A Moon Habitat of the Future
- Rockets will transport lightweight building materials from Earth.
- The construction materials will protect inhabitants from radiation and solar winds.
- The Sun will supply power for electricity.
- Technicians will use robots to mine the Moon's natural resources.
- More than one country will share the costs.

E GRAMMAR PRACTICE Read the predictions and complete the statements, putting each prediction into the future perfect in the passive voice. Then, with a partner, discuss the possible downsides to each prediction—or whether you think the good outweighs the bad. Explain your views.

Prediction 1: High-speed maglev trains will replace air travel as the preferred means of transportation.
Maglev trains, which use magnets and can travel at up to 580 kilometers per hour, are already preferred over air travel for many key European routes such as London-Paris. Will they replace even more routes? Some say it's not a question of if, but when.

By the end of the 21st century, ...
....
....
....

Prediction 2: Alternative methods of identification will replace passports for international travel.
Customs agencies will require cards with electronic chips that can be easily swiped, or perhaps they will rely on fingerprints to identify travelers. No matter how you look at it, stamping a passport is a thing of the past.

By the second half of the 21st century, ...
....
....
....

Prediction 3: Drone technology will make airplane pilots obsolete.
Would you fly on a pilotless plane? You may not have a choice. Once drones have become widely accepted, who needs pilots?

By 2075, ...
....
....
....

Prediction 4: A private company will construct a space hotel with a spectacular view of the Earth.
Got money to burn? How about a vacation in outer space? After decades of experience maintaining the International Space Station, a space hotel is the next logical step. Only the wealthy will be able to afford it. But what a view!

By the year 2100, ...
....
....
....

NOW YOU CAN Discuss the feasibility of future technologies

A NOTEPADDING On your notepad, write at least three wild predictions about the future, using the passive voice of <u>will</u> or <u>be going to</u> or the future perfect.

In the future	By 2050	By the end of the century

B DISCUSSION ACTIVATOR What future technologies do you think will catch on? Are you optimistic or pessimistic about the use of science and technology in the future? Why? Use the predictions on your notepad. Say as much as you can.

A ▶5:04 **VOCABULARY**   INNOVATIVE TECHNOLOGIES
Read and listen. Then listen again and repeat.

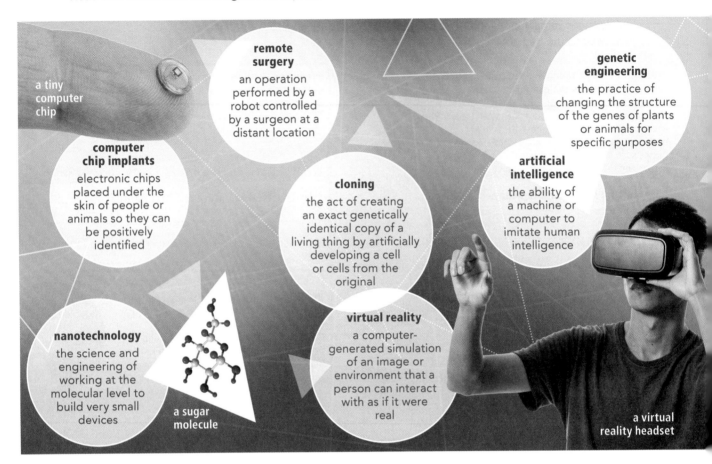

remote surgery
an operation performed by a robot controlled by a surgeon at a distant location

a tiny computer chip

computer chip implants
electronic chips placed under the skin of people or animals so they can be positively identified

genetic engineering
the practice of changing the structure of the genes of plants or animals for specific purposes

artificial intelligence
the ability of a machine or computer to imitate human intelligence

cloning
the act of creating an exact genetically identical copy of a living thing by artificially developing a cell or cells from the original

nanotechnology
the science and engineering of working at the molecular level to build very small devices

a sugar molecule

virtual reality
a computer-generated simulation of an image or environment that a person can interact with as if it were real

a virtual reality headset

B ▶5:05 **LISTEN TO ACTIVATE VOCABULARY**   Listen to conversations about applications of innovative technologies. After each, write the technology they're discussing, using the Vocabulary. Listen again and describe how the technology is being used.

	Innovative technology	How it's being used
1		
2		
3		
4		
5		
6		
7		

C ▶5:06 **LISTEN TO IDENTIFY POINT OF VIEW**   Listen again. Circle whether the speaker is for or against each technology. Then, with a partner, explain each answer.

1 He's (for / against) it.
2 She's (for / against) it.
3 She's (for / against) it.

4 She's (for / against) it.
5 She's (for / against) it.

6 He's (for / against) it.
7 They're (for / against) it.

D GRAMMAR   THE PASSIVE VOICE IN UNREAL CONDITIONAL SENTENCES

The present unreal conditional

If effective cancer-fighting drugs **were developed** through genetic engineering, that technology **might be** more widely **accepted**.

Note: The passive voice can be used in one or both clauses in an unreal conditional sentence.

The past unreal conditional

If antibiotics **had been discovered** earlier, the death toll from pneumonia might have been lower.
If the computer chip **hadn't been developed**, smartphones and tablets **would** never **have been invented**.

E GRAMMAR PRACTICE   Read the true statements. Then, on a separate sheet of paper, write unreal conditional statements with your own opinions, using the passive voice in <u>if</u> clauses.

Example: Operations aren't always performed by robots.

1 Chips aren't implanted in our bodies at birth.

2 Genetic engineering isn't prohibited.

If operations were always performed by robots, there would never be any surgical errors.

3 Human cloning isn't permitted.

4 The airplane was invented in the early 1900s.

5 The dinosaur was made extinct.

6 Written language was developed thousands of years ago.

7 Electricity was discovered in the seventeenth century.

F PAIR WORK   Compare the seven opinions you wrote for Exercise E with a partner. Explain your opinions, providing examples.

NOW YOU CAN   Evaluate applications of innovative technologies

A ▶5:07 CONVERSATION SPOTLIGHT   Read and listen. Notice the spotlighted conversation strategies.

A: I've been thinking about it and this human cloning sounds like a good thing to me. **For one thing**, couples who weren't able to have kids would finally be able to.

B: Well, if you ask me, I think it's pretty scary.

A: Really? What makes you say that?

B: It's a slippery slope. **I mean**, before you know it, someone's going to use it for something bad, like making designer babies.

A: I see your point. But people have always worried about new things.

▶5:09 **Ways to express a concern about consequences**
It's a slippery slope.
It's like opening a can of worms.
It's like playing with fire.
It's like opening Pandora's box.

B ▶5:08 RHYTHM AND INTONATION   Listen again and repeat. Then practice the conversation with a partner.

C NOTEPADDING   On your notepad, write an innovative technology that exists in the present and one you'd like to see in the future. Write one important application or use of each technology.

Present technology	Application
genetic engineering	create disease-resistant seeds

Present technology	Application

Future technology	Application

D CONVERSATION ACTIVATOR   Create a conversation similar to the one in Exercise A, using one of the innovative technologies on your notepad. Start like this: *I've been thinking about it and ___ sounds ___ to me.* Be sure to change roles and then partners.

DON'T STOP!

- Provide more reasons you are for or against a particular technology.
- Evaluate applications of other technologies.
- Say as much as you can.

A **READING WARM-UP** What threats today will affect the environment of the future?

DIGITAL STRATEGIES **B** ▶ 5:10 **READING** Read the article. What environmental threats does it address?

ORDINARY PEOPLE WITH BIG IDEAS— PRACTICAL STRATEGIES TO PROTECT THE EARTH

All around the globe, there are quiet hard-working people doing what it takes to protect our environment. They are changing minds and attitudes and demonstrating that ordinary people can make a difference.

HERE ARE TWO INSPIRING STORIES.

▲ California's huge redwoods

REVERSING GLOBAL WARMING ONE TREE AT A TIME

Old-growth forests play a key role in keeping the earth's atmosphere clean. In these forests, most trees are over 100 years old—many even 1,000 years or more. Unfortunately, after centuries of logging, development, pollution, and disease, about 98% of these forests have been destroyed, contributing to global warming. However, David Milarch and Leslie Lee, co-founders of a U.S. environmental group called Archangel Ancient Tree Archive, are doing something to turn things around.

Tree experts told him it couldn't be done, but Milarch and his sons, Jared and Jake, have been cloning trees from among more than sixty of the world's best-known, oldest, and largest species, creating exact copies of these ancient trees. These include California's huge redwoods and sequoias (some are 2,000 to 3,000 years old!), Ireland's imposing ancient oaks, and Lebanon's historic cedars.

Milarch and Lee want people to buy their cloned trees and plant them—millions of them. The trees then can produce oxygen, which is good for the environment; absorb carbon, which is bad for the environment; and in some cases even be used in the manufacture of much-needed medications. Eventually Milarch hopes to clone over 200 different species and return some of the old-growth forests we have lost through human activity. "I'm a workaholic. I work 16 hours a day, 365 days a year," says Milarch. When asked how he wants to be remembered, he says, "He caused us to stop and think and take action."

◀ David Milarch

PROTECTING WILDLIFE BY CHANGING MINDS

Cambodia is experiencing a rise in population and unregulated development, which has been destructive for the environment. More and more inexperienced farmers are taking up agriculture near the edges of Cambodia's forests. Unfortunately for Cambodia's wild Asian elephants, this has caused a conflict with humans. As elephants search for food, they have destroyed farms. In turn, poor and uneducated farmers have killed the elephants to protect their livelihoods. By the early years of this century, the population of elephants had fallen dramatically from about 2,000 to 500.

Tuy Sereivathana (known as Vathana) grew up in the countryside, where he learned to respect both nature and the elephants. After choosing to study forestry, he committed himself to conservation of Cambodia's natural resources. Eventually, working for the country's national parks, he focused his attention on understanding the problems the Cambodian farmers were facing.

Vathana realized that the farmers needed to know more about the elephants' migration patterns and how to apply practical solutions for protecting their farms. He helped them build electric fences. He taught them how to use hot chili peppers and other native plants that elephants don't like in order to discourage the animals from eating their crops. He convinced the farmers to organize themselves to guard their farms at night, using fireworks and other loud noises to scare the elephants off. He also helped them improve their farming techniques so they would not have to go farther into the elephants' habitat.

Vathana worked to establish community schools to increase literacy and provide wildlife conservation education. And he helped redevelop the cultural pride Cambodians have long had in their elephants. The farmers are now the elephants' greatest protectors. Vathana is now known as "Uncle Elephant." There has not been a single killing of a wild Asian elephant since 2005.

Tuy Sereivathana ▶

C **UNDERSTAND MEANING FROM CONTEXT**   Find the underlined words and phrases in the article. Then complete each statement. Explain your answers.

1 If you turn things around, it means you are making something ....

  a worse   b better   c stay the same

2 Redwoods, sequoias, oaks, and cedars are types of ....

  a clones   b trees   c medications

3 When trees absorb carbon, it is actually ....

  a good for the environment   b bad for the environment   c causing global warming

4 Unregulated development is ....

  a good for the environment   b bad for the environment   c good for farmers

5 If something falls dramatically, it means it ....

  a hasn't changed   b has changed a little   c has changed a lot

6 A native plant is one that has ...... another place.

  a been brought in from   b not been brought in from   c been cloned at

D **DRAW CONCLUSIONS**   In small groups, discuss the following questions. Find information in the article to support your answers.

1 What do old-growth forests do that's beneficial to this planet?

2 Why does Milarch focus specifically on cloning ancient tree species?

3 What were the benefits of Vathana's decision to work closely with the farmers?

DIGITAL EXTRA CHALLENGE
4 What might be a long-term benefit of teaching wildlife conservation in Cambodian schools?

NOW YOU CAN | Discuss how to protect our future environment

A **FRAME YOUR IDEAS**   Complete the questionnaire and compare answers with a partner. Which of you appears to be the more environmentally conscious?

HOW ENVIRONMENTALLY CONSCIOUS ARE YOU?
Check off the things that you do—and add some more.

TO REDUCE POLLUTION

☐ I use energy-efficient appliances.

☐ I use energy-efficient compact fluorescent light bulbs or LED bulbs instead of incandescent bulbs.

☐ I walk as often as I can or take public transportation instead of driving.

☐ And I ...

TO PRESERVE WATER

☐ I place a brick in the toilet's reservoir tank.

☐ I take showers instead of baths whenever I can.

☐ I turn off the water while I brush my teeth or shave.

☐ And I ...

TO AVOID WASTING FOOD

☐ I use leftovers to create new meals.

☐ I compost food to use in the garden.

☐ I only buy as much food as I need.

☐ And I ...

B **PRESENTATION**   In a small group, choose one of the three categories in the questionnaire. Develop an action plan and present it to your class.

GOAL Examine future social and demographic trends

DIGITAL STRATEGIES **A** ▶5:11 **LISTENING WARM-UP** VOCABULARY **DESCRIBING SOCIAL AND DEMOGRAPHIC TRENDS**
Read and listen. Then listen again and repeat.

dem·o·graph·ic /ˈdɛməˈgræfɪk ◀/ n. **1 demographics** [plural] information about the people who live in a particular area, such as how many people there are or what types of people there are: *the changing demographics of Southern California* **2** [singular] a part of the population that is considered as a group, especially for the purpose of advertising or trying to sell goods: *Cable television is focused on the 18 to 49 demographic (= people who are 18 to 49 years old).*

rate /reɪt/ n. [C] **1** the number of times something happens, or the number of examples of something within a certain period: **[+ of]** *The rate of new HIV infections has risen again.* | **at a rate of sth** *Refugees were crossing the border at a rate of 1,000 a day.* | *The unemployment rate rose to 6.5% in February.* | *The city still has a high crime rate.*

sta·tis·tic / stəˈtɪstɪk / n. **1 statistics** [plural] a collection of numbers which represents facts or measurements: *official crime statistics* **2** [singular] a single number which represents a fact or measurement: *a depressing statistic.* | **a statistic that** *I read a statistic that over 10,000 Americans a day turn 50.*

trend / trɛnd / n. [C] a general tendency in the way a situation is changing or developing: *Social and economic trends affect everyone.* | **[+ in]** *The researchers studied trends in drug use among teenagers.* | **[+ toward]** *There is a worldwide trend toward smaller families.* | *Davis is hoping to **reverse the trend** of rising taxes (= make a trend go in the opposite direction).* | **a current / recent / present trend** *If current trends continue, tourism will increase by 10%.* | *There is a growing trend in the country toward buying organic foods.*

Excerpted from Longman Advanced American Dictionary

B **APPLY THE VOCABULARY** Write whether each example is a demographic, a statistic, a rate, or a trend. Explain your choices.

1 An increasing number of customers are choosing to stream movies at home rather than go to a theater to see them. ....

2 The social media site *Pinterest* is used by more women than men. ....

3 The number of births per family is lower in wealthier developed countries. ....

4 Fifteen percent of seniors in the U.S. are living in poverty. ....

DIGITAL STRATEGIES **C** ▶5:12 **LISTEN TO ACTIVATE VOCABULARY** Listen to people discussing demographic trends. Write the number of the conversation next to the rate (or rates) they are discussing. (One rate is not discussed at all.) Then circle whether the rate is rising or falling. Listen again to check your work.

▶5:13 **Listen and repeat.**
literacy = ability to read and write
fertility = ability to reproduce
mortality = death

☐ **crime rate**	(rising / falling)	☐ **literacy rate**	(rising / falling)
☐ **birthrate**	(rising / falling)	☐ **fertility rate**	(rising / falling)
☐ **mortality rate**	(rising / falling)	☐ **divorce rate**	(rising / falling)

D ▶5:14 **LISTEN TO CONFIRM CONTENT**
Now listen to a lecture predicting world population trends. Read the list of subjects. Then listen again and check the subjects that were mentioned.

■ a decrease in world population
■ unemployment rates
■ life expectancy
■ marriage trends
■ divorce rates
■ fertility rates
■ mortality rates
■ literacy rates

E ▶ 5:15 **LISTEN TO INFER INFORMATION**   Read the statements. Then listen to the lecture again. Circle the word or phrase that best completes each statement, according to the information presented in the lecture.

1 According to the U.N. report, if the world's fertility and infant mortality rates don't decrease, the world's population will increase by (less than / more than / approximately) 30% by 2040.

2 By 2050, the country with the second highest population in the world will be (China / India / the U.S.).

3 By 2050, populations in Japan, Russia, and Germany will be (higher / lower / the same).

4 Worldwide, the number of older people will be (the same as / lower than / higher than) the number of younger people.

5 In 2050, the total number of children in the continent of Africa will be (lower than / higher than / the same as) the total number in the rest of the world.

F **SUPPORT AN OPINION**   Which of the statistics about future world demographics concern you the most? Explain your reasons.

NOW YOU CAN   Examine future social and demographic trends

A **NOTEPADDING**   With a partner, examine some social and demographic trends in your country that concern you. Write them on your notepad. Decide which of the trends present the greatest challenges.

> Marriage and divorce: *Fewer and fewer people are getting married.*

Marriage and divorce:	
Government and politics:	
The news media:	
Education:	
Family life:	
Seniors:	
Other:	

B **DISCUSSION**   Discuss with your partner some possible solutions to meet the challenges you identified in Exercise A. Then present your ideas to your class and invite your classmates to share their own ideas.

OPTIONAL WRITING   On a separate sheet of paper, write three paragraphs about one of the trends you discussed. In the first paragraph, explain the problem and give examples. In the second paragraph, explain the challenges. In the third, suggest some solutions.

A **WRITING SKILL** Study the rules.

A formal essay should include a thesis statement somewhere in the introductory paragraph. The thesis statement presents an argument or point of view. The supporting paragraphs should be organized to provide reasons, facts, or examples to support your thesis. The outline on the left indicates an effective way to organize a formal essay to support a thesis.

To write a thesis statement …
• Narrow the topic to one or two main ideas.
• Make sure it expresses your point of view.

WRITING MODEL

In twenty years, cars will probably all be powered by alternative energy sources, and they will be equipped with new technologies that take over many of the responsibilities of driving. There are good reasons to be optimistic about these predictions since car manufacturers are already moving in this direction. Undoubtedly, new technological advances will make these developments almost certain to become reality.

I. Introductory paragraph (with a thesis statement)

Your introduction should include a thesis statement—a sentence that presents your argument. The remaining sentences should suggest what specific topics the essay will include.

Many experts predict that most cars of the future will be powered by electricity. Unlike today's electric cars, which have limitations that keep them from being as popular as gas-powered vehicles, electric cars in the future will be much easier to maintain. For example, …

II. Supporting paragraphs (with supporting examples)

Each supporting paragraph should include a topic sentence that supports your thesis statement, followed by supporting examples.

Advances in computing will also make human drivers obsolete. Cars of the future will have advanced technological features, some of which are being applied today, that do the thinking for the driver. First of all, cars will all be able to park themselves. In addition, …

III. Concluding paragraph (with a summary)

Your conclusion should summarize the main points of the entire essay and restate your thesis.

Based on the direction the car industry is heading today, we can confidently predict some of the key advances we will see in the cars of the future. The industry is already offering both electric and hybrid vehicles, and it has introduced some "driverless" features, so we can expect much more development in those two areas.

B **PRACTICE** Essay tests often suggest topics in the form of a question. On a separate sheet of paper, write a thesis statement for each topic. Be sure to apply the guidelines above.

1 How can we end poverty?

> *Poverty can only be ended if the government makes that one of its highest priorities.*

2 Are hospitals and medical care getting too expensive?

3 How are fast-food restaurants changing the way people eat?

4 What are the best ways to avoid becoming a crime victim?

5 Do video games affect young people in negative ways?

6 What are the best places to go on vacation?

DIGITAL WRITING PROCESS

C **APPLY THE WRITING SKILL**

Write a four- or five-paragraph essay on one of the suggested topics. State your argument in the introduction with a thesis statement. Support your argument with two or three supporting paragraphs. In your conclusion, restate your argument and summarize the main points.

Suggested topics
• Transportation in the future
• Communication in the future
• Health care in the future
• Education in the future
• The future of the earth
• Your own idea: ....

SELF-CHECK

☐ Does my thesis statement clearly state my argument?

☐ Does each of my supporting paragraphs have a topic sentence that supports my point of view?

☐ Does my conclusion summarize my main points and restate my thesis?

A ▶5:16 **Listen to the conversations. Complete each statement with the technology the people are referring to and circle the word or phrase that reflects each person's opinion.**

1 He's (skeptical / excited) about ....

2 She (doesn't think / thinks) .... is a great idea.

3 He's (skeptical / excited) about ....

4 He's (bothered / not bothered) by ....

B **Write statements, using the underlined idioms in your statements.**

1 something you think is going to <u>catch on</u> in the future

....

2 something that would be like <u>opening a can of worms</u>

....

3 a situation in which someone <u>turned things around</u>

....

> *I'm certain that home delivery of restaurant meals using drones will catch on someday.*

C **Complete the paragraph with words and phrases from the list. Make any necessary changes.**

trend	statistics	mortality rate	birthrate	population growth	demographic

.... indicate that there are over 6 billion people in the world, with an increase of a
(1)

million people each year. This .... is not a result of an increased .... In fact, the
(2)   (3)

worldwide .... is for women to have fewer children. This increase in population is mainly the
(4)

result of a decrease in the child .... with more children living to adulthood. People are living
(5)

much longer lives. When the first humans walked the earth, the average person lived only to the age of

twenty. Today, the senior .... is rapidly increasing in size, especially in developing countries.
(6)

D **Rewrite each of the following sentences in the passive voice. Do not include a <u>by</u> phrase.**

1 In two years, engineers will have designed a new factory.

....

2 Engineers are going to equip the factory with air filters.

....

3 Workers will recycle paper, metal, and plastic.

....

4 They're going to treat waste before they release it into rivers.

....

5 New technologies are going to reduce energy demands by 50 percent.

....

6 Pipes will collect rainwater, and they will transport it to tanks.

....

7 Pipes will also carry excess heat from one building to another.

....

TEST-TAKING SKILLS BOOSTER p. 159

Web Project: Animal Conservation
www.english.com/summit3e

An Interconnected World

COMMUNICATION GOALS

1 React to news about global issues
2 Describe the impact of foreign imports
3 Discuss the pros and cons of globalization
4 Suggest ways to avoid culture shock

PREVIEW

A FRAME YOUR IDEAS   Complete the quiz.

GET THE FACTS!

Test your knowledge about English in today's world.

1 English is NOT an official language in ....
☐ Canada
☐ the U.S. or the U.K.
☐ South Africa
☐ Nigeria

2 There are approximately ...... people in the world who can speak English.
☐ 1.5 million
☐ 10 million
☐ 1 billion
☐ 1.5 billion

3 Approximately ...... of the world's population are native speakers of English.
☐ 5%
☐ 10%
☐ 20%
☐ 30%

4 There are about ...... million people who speak English as a foreign language.
☐ 6
☐ 10
☐ 70
☐ 700

5 ...... is the country with the most English speakers.
☐ China
☐ the U.S.
☐ the U.K.
☐ India

6 Approximately ...... million children are studying English in China.
☐ 1
☐ 10
☐ 100
☐ 500

7 In France, there are approximately ...... post-secondary degree programs offered in English.
☐ 20
☐ 100
☐ 300
☐ 700

8 Approximately ...... of the information stored in the world's computers is in English.
☐ 10%
☐ 30%
☐ 50%
☐ 80%

9 Approximately ...... new words are added to the English language each year.
☐ 10
☐ 100
☐ 400
☐ 4,000

ANSWERS   1. Neither the U.S. nor the U.K. has an official language. English is the main language in those countries by history and tradition. Both English and French are official languages in Canada. South Africa has 11 official languages, including English. Nigeria has only one—English.   **2.** According to some estimates, 1.5 billion people in the world speak English—that's one out of every six people, and the number is growing.   **3.** There are about 380 million native speakers of English, a little over 5% of the world's population.   **4.** There are anywhere from 700 million to one billion people who have learned—or are currently learning—English in addition to their own language.   **5.** The U.S. has the most English speakers, native and non-native, at 298 million. Ranking highest after that are India (125 million), Pakistan (92 million), Nigeria (82 million), and the U.K. (64 million). But there are more English speakers in Asia than in the U.S., U.K., and Canada combined.   **6.** 100 million children are learning English in China. That's more than the population of the U.K.   **7.** French universities offer 700 degree programs in English. France attracts more foreign university students than any other non-English-speaking country.   **8.** Eighty percent of the world's digitally stored information is in English, but the proportion of information stored in other languages is growing.   **9.** Four thousand new words are added yearly, making English the language with the largest vocabulary in the world.

B PAIR WORK   Did any of the answers surprise you? Explain why or why not.

C ▶ 5:17 **SPOTLIGHT**   Read and listen to a conversation about someone's plans. Notice the spotlighted language.

> **Paul:** Are you still thinking about going overseas for a master's program?
>
> **Hyo:** Actually, I've been checking out engineering programs in both Los Angeles and London. But I guess I'm still **on the fence**—I haven't made up my mind which I prefer.
>
> **Paul:** Well, why don't you check out ECE Paris? They have a top-notch engineering program.
>
> **Hyo:** Are you serious? **It's bad enough that** I wouldn't be able to handle the coursework in French. But between the culture shock and not being able to use my English there, I'd feel like **a fish out of water**.
>
> **Paul:** Well, believe it or not, they're offering their engineering program in English.
>
> **Hyo:** In Paris? You**'re pulling my leg**, right?
>
> **Paul:** No way! I kid you not.
>
> **Hyo:** No offense, Paul, but isn't France like the *last* place you'd expect anyone to be offering classes in English? I heard the French government actually tried to keep all university instruction in French.
>
> **Paul:** That was probably true some years ago, but I guess they decided it was **a losing battle**. Apparently universities *had* to offer classes in English in order to continue attracting students from abroad—like you!
>
> **Hyo:** **How do you like that!** I guess **money talks** ...
>
> **Paul:** At any rate, I'm sure you'd fall in love with my hometown. And besides, you could pick up some French while you're there.

D **UNDERSTAND IDIOMS AND EXPRESSIONS 1**   Circle the correct word or phrase to complete each explanation.

1 If you're "on the fence," you haven't (made a decision / changed your plans).
2 If you feel like "a fish out of water," everything seems (exciting / unfamiliar) to you.
3 If someone "pulls your leg," he or she is (being serious / only kidding).
4 If something is "a losing battle," it's probably best to (give up / keep trying).

E **UNDERSTAND IDIOMS AND EXPRESSIONS 2**   Complete each statement with the correct lettered explanation.

1 When Hyo says "It's bad enough that ... ," he's ......
2 When Hyo says "How do you like that!" he's ......
3 When Hyo says "Money talks," he's ......

a emphasizing a problem.
b offering an explanation.
c expressing surprise.

F **THINK AND EXPLAIN**   With a partner, discuss the questions and explain your answers.

1 Why does Paul suggest that Hyo study in Paris? What would be the benefits?
2 What explanation is Hyo offering when he says, "I guess money talks ... "?

SPEAKING   Read the opinions. Explain why you agree or disagree. Discuss how you think you will use English in your own lives.

If you want to be considered proficient in English, you should never make mistakes, and you should sound like a native speaker.	These days, speaking English is like knowing how to use a computer—you need both skills for a better job.	The most important goal in learning English is to be able to function socially and communicate successfully.	I think the only real reason to learn English is to travel or work overseas. If those aren't your plans, it's not particularly useful.

GOAL React to news about global issues

DIGITAL STRATEGIES

A ▶ 5:18 **VOCABULARY** PHRASAL VERBS* TO DISCUSS ISSUES AND PROBLEMS
Read and listen. Then listen again and repeat.

bring about make something happen; to cause to occur or exist

We need to agree about what the problems are if we expect to bring about changes.

carry out achieve or accomplish a plan or project

It's time the president carried out her promise to vaccinate all school-age children.

come down with become sick with a particular illness

More than a million people have come down with the mosquito-borne virus.

come up with think of something such as an idea or a plan

Municipal governments need to come up with a new approach to reduce homelessness.

go without live without something you need or usually have

No one should have to go without clean drinking water.

lay off end the employment of workers due to economic conditions

The company recently announced they were laying off two hundred employees.

put up with accept a bad situation or person without complaining

For many years, people in small villages have put up with inadequate roads.

run out of use up all of something and not have any more of it

If we're not careful, we'll run out of oil before alternative energy sources have been found.

wipe out end or destroy something completely so it no longer exists

Ten years ago, few people could read or write in this country, but now illiteracy has been nearly wiped out.

***Remember:** Phrasal verbs contain a verb and one or more particles that together have their own meaning. Particles are most commonly prepositions and adverbs.*

B ▶ 5:19 **LISTEN TO ACTIVATE VOCABULARY**
Listen to the conversations about global issues. After each conversation, complete the statement.

Conversation 1 The refugees will ....

  a go without food soon   **b** come down with something   **c** carry out a plan

Conversation 2 Lots of people have been ....

  a putting up with vaccinations   **b** coming down with the disease   **c** coming up with a plan

Conversation 3 The government hasn't ....

  a carried out the president's plan yet   **b** run out of supplies   **c** laid off anyone

C **VOCABULARY PRACTICE 1** Circle the correct phrasal verb to complete each sentence.

1 Because of increased availability of the flu vaccine this year, very few people have (come up with / come down with) the disease.

2 Many believe that it is essential to (carry out / wipe out) terrorist organizations.

3 A decrease in donations to humanitarian organizations will force thousands to (go without / put up with) the food they need to survive.

4 The oil company claims it will have to (bring about / lay off) one-third of its workforce on three continents.

5 Attempts to help the earthquake survivors were successful until the United Nations relief agencies (ran out of / laid off) supplies.

6 Change was (brought about / run out of) through the work of volunteers.

7 City residents will have to (put up with / lay off) the presence of foreign military troops.

8 Hopefully someone will (put up with / come up with) a plan to reverse global warming.

9 The actress's volunteer work is helping human rights groups (wipe out / carry out) their mission to help war refugees settle into their new lives overseas.

D VOCABULARY PRACTICE 2 Complete the article, using the appropriate forms of the phrasal verbs.

UN HUNGER RELIEF

The UN World Food Program (WFP) is the world's largest humanitarian organization dealing with the issue of hunger and how to **(1)** _____ malnutrition, especially among children. Its goal is to **(2)** _____ improvements in food production and to **(3)** _____ its plans to provide food assistance to millions of people in seventy-five countries around the world. Whenever people are forced to **(4)** _____ food because of droughts or war, the WFP tries to help. Under these famine conditions, people are unable to feed their families and they are forced to **(5)** _____ being hungry on a daily basis. Making the situation worse, many of its malnourished victims are more vulnerable due to weakened immune systems and may **(6)** _____ contagious diseases. It is the WFP's responsibility to make sure that relief groups do not **(7)** _____ essential emergency supplies. In the 1990s, the WFP **(8)** _____ a successful money-saving idea for responding more quickly to emergencies using small teams of experts to assess the situation before committing full-scale resources.

NOW YOU CAN React to news about global issues

A ▶ 5:20 CONVERSATION SPOTLIGHT Read and listen.
Notice the spotlighted conversation strategies.

A: **Can you believe** what's been happening in Northern Africa?
B: You mean the drought? It's just horrendous.
A: Awful. **But on the bright side**, people have been donating tons of money for relief. I find that really inspiring.
B: Totally. **It just goes to show you** how powerful social media can be.
A: But on the other hand, it's appalling how much corruption there is.
B: **Well, that's another story** … It makes you feel hopeless, doesn't it?
A: Yeah. **You'd think** someone could do something to stop it.

B ▶ 5:21 RHYTHM AND INTONATION Listen again and repeat.
Then practice the conversation with a partner.

C CONVERSATION ACTIVATOR Create a similar conversation,
using one of these news stories. Start like this: *Can you believe …?* Be sure to change roles and then partners.

DIGITAL VIDEO
DIGITAL SPEAKING BOOSTER

DON'T STOP!
- Describe the news in more detail.
- Say more about your response to the news.
- Say as much as you can.

RECYCLE THIS LANGUAGE
- It's a slippery slope. / It's like opening a can of worms.
- The good outweighs the bad.
- Before you know it, …
- Don't get me wrong.
- What [bothers / concerns] me is …

PRONUNCIATION BOOSTER p. 150
Intonation of tag questions

Celebrities Raise Millions for Famine Victims

The North African drought has forced four million people to go without adequate food and water. Some of the world's best-known celebrities have come up with a plan to use social media to raise money for humanitarian efforts.

TERRORIST ATTACK ATTRACTS INTERNATIONAL ACTIVISM

After hearing about the bombing in Beirut that left forty dead, Colombian businesswoman Leticia Gómez decided to use her connections to carry out a campaign to help the families of the victims. Gómez lost her husband to a bombing in Bogotá in the eighties and knows firsthand how devastating terrorism can be.

STEPS TAKEN TO AVOID EPIDEMIC IN THE PHILIPPINES

Hundreds have come down with an unknown illness in Mindanao, causing authorities to restrict both domestic and international travel. Doctors Without Borders has agreed to send a team to investigate.

China Carries Out Conference Recommendations

The government has come up with a long-term plan for reducing factory emissions in China, where urban residents have had to put up with high levels of pollution with its resulting health consequences.

GOAL Describe the impact of foreign imports

A ▶ 5:22 **GRAMMAR SPOTLIGHT** Read the people's opinions and notice the spotlighted grammar.

"I do a lot of business travel, and it's amazing how you **run into** so many foreign things—for example, a Starbucks coffee shop from the U.S. in Bogotá, Colombia. Hello! Colombia already *has* great coffee! Recently I **came across** the Japanese clothing chain UNIQLO in New York. Almost everywhere you go now, you can **count on** being able to find a restaurant that serves Indian, Thai, Japanese, or Mexican food. In any city, people can **take up** tai chi from China, yoga from India, or capoeira from Brazil. Seems like every place is becoming the same."

Gina Falcone, U.S.

"Every time my kids **turn** their tablets or smartphones **on**, I worry. I'm concerned about the influence foreign games and websites will have on them. I don't particularly **care for** some of the values they teach. But my kids are crazy about their gadgets. If I were to ask my kids to **give** them **up**, I'd never hear the end of it! They can't imagine **going without** them. I've been trying to **talk** them **into** doing other things, but it's a bit of a losing battle, I'm afraid. I guess I just have to learn to **put up with** their devices."

Mehmet Demirkahn, Turkey

"Nowadays you see foreign brands everywhere you look. Before you **throw** the packaging from a food item **away**, read the label—it might say it comes from the U.S. or Mexico. **Try** a blouse **on** at the store—nine times out of ten, it'll have come from China, Vietnam, or Bangladesh. Or **try** some new product **out** at the electronics store and there's a good chance it's imported from Korea. Some people worry that imports will **wipe out** our own local products. But the way I see it, we can enjoy foreign things and still value and appreciate our own."

Sophia Freitas, Brazil

B **ACTIVATE PRIOR KNOWLEDGE** Would people in your country express opinions similar to the ones in the Grammar Spotlight? Explain.

> **GRAMMAR BOOSTER** p. 142
> Phrasal verbs: expansion

C **GRAMMAR** SEPARABILITY OF TRANSITIVE PHRASAL VERBS

Remember: Transitive verbs are verbs that can have direct objects. Transitive *phrasal verbs* can be separable or inseparable.

Separable

A direct object noun can generally come after or before the particle of a separable phrasal verb.

Check out their website. OR **Check** their website **out**.

However, a direct object pronoun must come before the particle.

Check it **out**. NOT ~~Check out it~~.

Inseparable

A direct object noun or pronoun always comes after the particle of an inseparable phrasal verb.

They **cater to** younger customers. NOT They ~~cater younger customers to~~.

I **ran into** her at the park. NOT I ~~ran her into~~ the park.

Be careful! Some phrasal verbs are always separated. The particle never comes directly after the verb.

I **talked** them **into** contributing money. NOT I ~~talked into them~~ contributing money.

Separable			
bring about	give up	wipe out	turn on / off
carry out	lay off	try on	throw away
figure out	pick up	try out	
find out	take up		

Inseparable		
care for	come down with	put up with
cater to	count on	run into
come across	go after	run out of
come up with	go without	

Always separated

do (sth.) over   start (sth.) over   talk (s.o.) into (sth.)

For a complete list with definitions, see pp. 124–126.

D UNDERSTAND THE GRAMMAR   Which phrasal verbs in the Grammar Spotlight are separable? Rewrite each of those sentences, with the direct object in a different position.

E GRAMMAR PRACTICE   Complete the sentences, using a form of the phrasal verb with the pronoun it or <u>them</u>. Pay attention to whether or not the phrasal verb is separable.

1 Yoga is really popular. Even my great-grandmother has (take up) ....
2 Although only a small minority of the population can understand English, English words are visible everywhere. You often (come across) .... on signs, product ads, and even clothing.
3 The workers who have been laid off have highly developed skills. It may not be so easy to (talk into) .... learning all new skills.
4 Because young adults are tech-savvy and have tremendous economic power, many Internet companies have developed marketing campaigns that (go after) .... exclusively.
5 At the International Trade Fair, foreign companies offer samples of their products. People can (try out) .... before deciding whether to buy them.
6 Once a foreign brand has become popular, it's hard to for people to (give up) ....

NOW YOU CAN   Describe the impact of foreign imports

A NOTEPADDING   On your notepad, list examples of imports from foreign countries or cultures that you come across regularly.

B DISCUSSION ACTIVATOR   Have the imports you listed on your notepad had a positive or negative impact? Explain, providing examples. Say as much as you can.

C PAIR WORK   Read the statements about foreign imports. Discuss whether you agree or disagree with them, providing examples. Use phrasal verbs when you can.

Foods:	Entertainment:
Music:	Vehicles:
Products for your home:	Sports and games:
Clothing / personal accessories:	Other:

> There's a growing trend towards **giving up** local traditions and replacing them with imported things. But I question the wisdom of just **throwing away** our long-held traditions like that.

> Young people **are picking up** values from foreign media, so culturally we're becoming more and more alike. I wonder what would happen if we lose the things that make us different.

Hip-hop style has gone international.

Chinese restaurants are popular in Peru.

People dance salsa in Japan.

115

A **READING WARM-UP** Do people in your country generally view increased international trade positively or negatively? Explain.

B ▶ 5:23 **READING** Read the article on the effects of globalization. Do you share its concerns? Why or why not?

DIGITAL
STRATEGIES

GLOBALIZATION

DOES IT LIVE UP TO EXPECTATIONS?

Globalization and increased free trade in this century have brought the world's cultures and economies together. We depend more than ever on each other to thrive. Along with advances in technology and communication, we have become more interconnected as people, corporations, and brands travel across borders more easily than ever before. Nevertheless, most people agree that the social, economic, environmental, and political changes caused by globalization have brought both positive and negative results.

THE PROMISE

Advocates of globalization believed it would make the world smaller and bring diverse people and cultures closer. They were right. People in cities on opposite sides of the world can easily get in touch by phone, e-mail, instant messaging, or teleconference. Ease of communication and freer global trade have resulted in improved efficiency and competition. Companies are able to respond quickly to economic changes and market demands. As cooperation—and competition— have increased, new technologies are shared and developed.

Many countries have experienced improvements in their standard of living. For many people, an economic benefit of increased imports and exports has been an increase in income. Consumers enjoy a wider variety of choices when they shop. And as a result of increased prosperity, it has been possible to increase investment in new infrastructure—roads, bridges, and buildings.

THE OTHER SIDE OF THE STORY

While globalization promised to benefit everyone with an increase in worldwide wealth and prosperity, critics cite evidence of a widening gap between rich and poor. In developed countries, such as the U.S., corporations outsource both manufacturing and customer service jobs to developing countries in Asia and Latin America, where labor costs are lower. For example, India's economy benefits from the establishment of call centers, where English-speaking staff provide 24/7 technical support by phone and Internet to customers all over the world. Their technicians can do so at about one-fifth the cost of what companies would have to pay workers in developed economies for the same service. So while Indian workers benefit, workers in other countries complain that their jobs have been taken away.

Critics of globalization argue that free trade has made the world so competitive that criminal activities have flourished. For example, child labor, which is illegal in many countries, has increased to fill manufacturing demands for gold and textiles. Recent news reports have exposed the use of slavery on merchant ships, where workers are mistreated and forced to work without receiving any wages. Economic opportunities made possible by globalization have also encouraged corruption, in which government officials agree to ignore unethical business practices. Some argue that a global economy has helped drug cartels and terrorists move people and materials across borders more easily.

As internationally recognized fast-food chains have expanded throughout the world, critics complain that the fried foods and sugary drinks they serve have been replacing healthier local eating traditions and increasing the consumption of unhealthy junk food among young people. Some argue that globalization has led to a homogenization of culture in general—that local traditions are quickly being replaced by imported ones.

Even worse, without international regulation, developing countries such as Nigeria are becoming dumping grounds for hazardous industrial waste. In other countries such as China, increased development has brought with it uncontrolled pollution, reaching sky-high levels that threaten public health and contribute to global warming. And globalization has also been a strain on the environment as more and more natural resources are tapped for manufacturing.

Obviously, we can't turn back the clock on globalization. And we know that those countries that have embraced it have experienced increased economic growth. However, it is also clear that there are challenges to overcome despite globalization's many benefits.

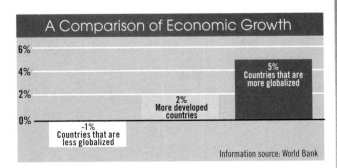

A Comparison of Economic Growth

6%
4%
2%
0%
-1%
Countries that are
less globalized

2%
More developed
countries

5%
Countries that are
more globalized

Information source: World Bank

C **UNDERSTAND MEANING FROM CONTEXT**   Match each word from the article with its definition.

...... **1** globalization
...... **2** exports
...... **3** investment
...... **4** infrastructure
...... **5** prosperity
...... **6** outsource
...... **7** homogenization

a money put into a company or business to encourage growth and make a profit
b the act of making it easier to produce products and trade them internationally
c products sold to other countries
d use other countries' services rather than one's own
e financial success
f things that make transport of products efficient
g causing things to become more similar

D **IDENTIFY SUPPORTING IDEAS**   Answer the questions, supporting your answers with information in the article.

1 What are some specific examples of both improved and decreased standard of living, caused by globalization?

2 What are some areas where businesses or governments could make investments that might address some of the challenges of globalization?

3 What are two examples given that describe workers who lose or are denied income?

4 What examples are given to illustrate the pros and cons of availability of foreign imports?

E **INTERPRET INFORMATION IN A GRAPH**   According to the graph, who benefits the most from globalization? Who benefits the least? Explain.

Increased imports and exports have led to economic growth in many countries.

NOW YOU CAN   Discuss the pros and cons of globalization

A **NOTEPADDING**   On your notepad, write the names of international companies that have had an economic, social, environmental, or political impact in your country.

B **DISCUSSION**   What benefits or problems have these companies brought to your country? Overall, do you think globalization is good or bad for your country? Explain.

have had an economic impact	have had a social impact
have had an environmental impact	have had a political impact

❝ Toyota's investment in local factories has been good for the country. It provides employment and pays good wages, raising the standard of living for a lot of people. ❞

Some well-known international companies
Apple
British Petroleum (BP)
IKEA

Nestle
Samsung
The Gap

117

GOAL Suggest ways to avoid culture shock

A **LISTENING WARM-UP** **DISCUSSION** Read the definition of culture shock. What feelings of anxiety or confusion might someone experiencing culture shock have? Give some examples of situations that might cause culture shock.

> **culture shock** *n.* the feelings of anxiety and confusion that people have when they visit a foreign country and experience a new culture for the first time

DIGITAL STRATEGIES **B** ▶ 5:24 **LISTEN TO SUMMARIZE** Listen to the radio program. In your own words, summarize the characteristics of each of the four stages of culture shock.

Susan Cahill

Stage one:

Stage two:

Stage three:

Berat Yildiz

Stage four:

C ▶ 5:25 **LISTEN TO CONFIRM INFORMATION** Listen again. Check the correct answers, according to the program.

1 Which of the following disorienting experiences did not cause negative feelings for Berat in London?

☐ the traffic ☐ the money ☐ the weather ☐ the food ☐ people's behavior

2 Which symptoms of culture shock did Berat experience?

☐ headaches ☐ disappointment ☐ sadness ☐ lack of sleep ☐ loneliness

3 Which of the following were mentioned as signs that Berat was in the final stage of culture shock?

☐ dressing right for cold weather ☐ making friends ☐ calling home
☐ appreciating cultural differences ☐ finding Turkish restaurants

LISTEN TO UNDERSTAND MEANING FROM CONTEXT Listen to the excerpts from the radio program. Use the context to help you complete each statement.

1 When Susan Cahill says that Berat Yildiz knows about culture shock "firsthand," she means he knows it from ....

   a experience   **b** his studies   **c** his culture

2 When Berat says he felt like he was "in heaven," he means he felt ....

   a worried   **b** shocked   **c** great

3 When Berat says he found some things "disorienting," he means he felt ....

   a comfortable   **b** confused   **c** angry

4 When Susan says there is "a light at the end of the tunnel," she means that things will ....

   a get better   **b** get worse   **c** stay the same

5 When Berat says he got his "feet back on the ground," he means he stopped ....

   a feeling confused   **b** feeling happy   **c** thinking about Turkish food

---

NOW YOU CAN Suggest ways to avoid culture shock

A **NOTEPADDING** Check the aspects of your culture you think might cause culture shock to a visitor to your country. Add others. Then choose the three from the list you think are the most difficult to deal with. Write notes suggesting ways to avoid the negative effects of each one.

1 ....

2 ....

3 ....

- [ ] local dishes
- [ ] eating and drinking customs
- [ ] the way people act at work
- [ ] greeting customs
- [ ] the way people socialize
- [ ] local holidays
- [ ] sense of humor
- [ ] formality and informality
- [ ] traditional leisure activities
- [ ] apologizing
- [ ] the do's and don'ts for clothing
- [ ] treatment of children
- [ ] customs for keeping pets
- [ ] how people shop
- [ ] public transportation
- [ ] driving or walking in traffic
- [ ] other ....
  ....

Try it. It's delicious!

B **PAIR WORK** Tell your partner why you chose the three topics. Describe your ideas for helping a visitor avoid the worst symptoms of culture shock.

OPTIONAL WRITING Write an article for visitors to this country, suggesting ways to be prepared for culture shock and avoid the most negative symptoms.

A WRITING SKILL Study the rules.

When writing a rebuttal to an opposing argument or point of view, support your ideas by presenting them one by one. Following is an outline to organize your essay effectively.

I. Introductory paragraph

Explain the issue and summarize the opposing point of view. Include a thesis statement stating your own point of view.

II. Supporting paragraphs

In each paragraph, state one aspect of the point of view you are rebutting. Use details and examples to support your own point of view.

III. Concluding paragraph

Summarize your point of view.

WRITING MODEL

I There are many people who feel that globalization is causing more problems than it is solving. **Nevertheless, it is my opinion that, overall, globalization has contributed to a better world.** We need to accept it as a reality of today's world and do what we can to make it work for everyone.

II **Critics argue that** many countries have not benefited as much as others. **All the same,** we shouldn't assume that all countries will benefit at the same speed or time. It is a fact that free trade has been a tremendous benefit to nations in East and Southeast Asia. Their economies have grown substantially in this century and their standard of living has greatly improved. There's no reason to believe this won't happen elsewhere, for example in West Africa.

It has been argued that globalization has increased the spread of disease, worsened pollution, and made it easier for criminals to cross borders. **In spite of this,** I believe that free trade and increased international cooperation have also made it easier for nations to fight these problems more effectively. With attention, these are problems that can be solved.

III Clearly, globalization has areas for improvement. **Even so, I believe the advantages of globalization far outweigh the problems.**

Expressions for introducing others' arguments:

According to [Bill Gates], ...
[Some people] say / think / feel that ...
[Many experts] argue / believe that ...
It may be true that ...
It has been argued / said / pointed out that ...

Transitions and subordinating conjunctions for your rebuttal:

However, ...   All the same, ...
Nevertheless, ...   In spite of this, ...
Even so, ...

B PRACTICE On a separate sheet of paper, write five sentences that introduce arguments for or against globalization. Paraphrase—using your own words—arguments from the article on page 116. Use the expressions for introducing others' arguments.

> People who defend globalization argue that the standard of living has improved in many countries.

C PRACTICE Now write statements to rebut each of the arguments opposing globalization that you introduced in Exercise B. Use the suggested transitions and subordinating conjunctions.

> Even so, it can be argued that too many countries have not enjoyed the benefits.

SELF-CHECK

- [ ] Did I summarize the point of view I want to rebut in my introduction?
- [ ] Did I rebut each argument by providing details and examples to support my own?
- [ ] Did I use the suggested expressions and transitions or subordinating conjunctions to link my ideas clearly?
- [ ] Did I summarize my point of view in my conclusion?

DIGITAL WRITING PROCESS

D APPLY THE WRITING SKILL Write an essay of at least four paragraphs in which you present your point of view about globalization and rebut the opposing point of view.

A ▶ 5:27 Listen to three news reports on globalization-related topics. After each report, complete each statement so that it is true, according to the information presented in the report. Listen again if necessary.

Report 1: WorldWatch is concerned that improving living standards in developing countries ....

   a will cause natural resources to run out
   b will bring about an increase in prices for luxury goods

Report 2: According to the report, most people think that globalization ....

   a is causing social and economic problems
   b is not causing social and economic problems

Report 3: The chairman of Starbucks believes that his customers appreciate ....

   a the convenience of having Starbucks stores in so many locations
   b both the coffee and the experience of being in the store

B Complete each phrasal verb with the correct particle. Use the phrasal verb list on pages 124–126 if necessary.

1 The island voted to carry .... the governor's plan to find foreign investors to develop the island into a tourist resort.

2 Technological advances such as social media have brought .... great changes in the way people communicate.

3 The president is determined to figure .... how to increase trade with other countries without causing a rise in unemployment.

4 Clerks were handing .... free cups of Colombian coffee at a Tokyo supermarket in the hopes that it would catch .... with local shoppers.

5 I picked .... a little French when I visited my uncle in Paris last summer, but I wouldn't say that I'm fluent.

6 A lot of families have been putting .... large purchases because they're afraid they may soon be out of work if the economy doesn't improve.

7 To be honest, I'm worried that the cultures of wealthier nations will one day wipe .... the traditional cultures of poorer nations.

8 Asian martial arts have become really popular recently. I know so many people who have taken .... tae kwon do, karate, or judo.

C On a separate sheet of paper, rewrite each sentence, replacing the underlined phrase with the pronoun it or them.

1 We should check out that new French film.

> *We should check it out.*

2 We're trying to go without imported products.
3 They voted to give up protections against imports.
4 Falling profits forced the factory owner to lay off the workers.
5 Just turn on your TV and you'll see news and films from all over the world.
6 I talked my friends into buying tickets for the U2 concert.
7 Manufacturers of luxury products cater to wealthier consumers.
8 If you take up karate, you'll probably be in great shape.

TEST-TAKING SKILLS BOOSTER p. 160

Web Project: Global Warming
www.english.com/summit3e

Reference Charts

base form	simple past	past participle	base form	simple past	past participle
be	was / were	been	mean	meant	meant
beat	beat	beaten	meet	met	met
become	became	become	mistake	mistook	mistaken
begin	began	begun	pay	paid	paid
bend	bent	bent	put	put	put
bet	bet	bet	quit	quit	quit
bite	bit	bitten	read /rid/	read /rɛd/	read /rɛd/
bleed	bled	bled	ride	rode	ridden
blow	blew	blown	ring	rang	rung
break	broke	broken	rise	rose	risen
breed	bred	bred	run	ran	run
bring	brought	brought	say	said	said
build	built	built	see	saw	seen
burn	burned / burnt	burned / burnt	sell	sold	sold
burst	burst	burst	send	sent	sent
buy	bought	bought	set	set	set
catch	caught	caught	shake	shook	shaken
choose	chose	chosen	shed	shed	shed
come	came	come	shine	shone	shone
cost	cost	cost	shoot	shot	shot
creep	crept	crept	show	showed	shown
cut	cut	cut	shrink	shrank	shrunk
deal	dealt	dealt	shut	shut	shut
dig	dug	dug	sing	sang	sung
do	did	done	sink	sank	sunk
draw	drew	drawn	sit	sat	sat
dream	dreamed / dreamt	dreamed / dreamt	sleep	slept	slept
drink	drank	drunk	slide	slid	slid
drive	drove	driven	smell	smelled / smelt	smelled / smelt
eat	ate	eaten	speak	spoke	spoken
fall	fell	fallen	speed	sped / speeded	sped / speeded
feed	fed	fed	spell	spelled / spelt	spelled / spelt
feel	felt	felt	spend	spent	spent
fight	fought	fought	spill	spilled / spilt	spilled / spilt
find	found	found	spin	spun	spun
fit	fit	fit	spit	spit / spat	spit / spat
fly	flew	flown	spoil	spoiled / spoilt	spoiled / spoilt
forbid	forbade	forbidden	spread	spread	spread
forget	forgot	forgotten	spring	sprang / sprung	sprang / sprung
forgive	forgave	forgiven	stand	stood	stood
freeze	froze	frozen	steal	stole	stolen
get	got	gotten	stick	stuck	stuck
give	gave	given	sting	stung	stung
go	went	gone	stink	stank / stunk	stunk
grow	grew	grown	strike	struck	struck / stricken
hang	hung	hung	string	strung	strung
have	had	had	swear	swore	sworn
hear	heard	heard	sweep	swept	swept
hide	hid	hidden	swim	swam	swum
hit	hit	hit	swing	swung	swung
hold	held	held	take	took	taken
hurt	hurt	hurt	teach	taught	taught
keep	kept	kept	tear	tore	torn
know	knew	known	tell	told	told
lay	laid	laid	think	thought	thought
lead	led	led	throw	threw	thrown
leap	leaped / leapt	leaped / leapt	understand	understood	understood
learn	learned / learnt	learned / learnt	upset	upset	upset
leave	left	left	wake	woke / waked	woken / waked
lend	lent	lent	wear	wore	worn
let	let	let	weave	wove	woven
lie	lay	lain	weep	wept	wept
light	lit	lit	win	won	won
lose	lost	lost	wind	wound	wound
make	made	made	write	wrote	written

VERBS FOLLOWED BY A GERUND

acknowledge	celebrate	discontinue	escape	imagine	postpone	recall	risk
admit	complete	discuss	explain	justify	practice	recommend	suggest
advise	consider	dislike	feel like	keep	prevent	report	support
appreciate	delay	don't mind	finish	mention	prohibit	resent	tolerate
avoid	deny	endure	forgive	mind	propose	resist	undestand
can't help	detest	enjoy	give up	miss	quit		

EXPRESSIONS THAT CAN BE FOLLOWED BY A GERUND

be excited about	be committed to	make an excuse for	look forward to
be worried about	be opposed to	have a reason for	blame [someone or something] for
be responsible for	be used to	believe in	forgive [someone or something] for
be interested in	complain about	participate in	thank [someone or something] for
be accused of	dream about / of	succeed in	keep [someone or something] from
be capable of	talk about / of	take advantage of	prevent [someone or something] from
be tired of	think about / of	take care of	stop [someone or something] from
be accustomed to	apologize for	insist on	

VERBS FOLLOWED DIRECTLY BY AN INFINITIVE

afford	can't wait	demand	hope	need	pretend	swear	want
agree	care	deserve	hurry	neglect	promise	threaten	wish
appear	choose	expect	intend	offer	refuse	volunteer	would like
arrange	claim	fail	learn	pay	request	wait	yearn
ask	consent	grow	manage	plan	seem		
attempt	decide	hesitate	mean	prepare	struggle		

VERBS FOLLOWED BY AN OBJECT BEFORE AN INFINITIVE*

advise	cause	enable	force	need*	persuade	require	want*
allow	challenge	encourage	hire	order	promise*	teach	warn
ask*	choose*	expect*	instruct	pay*	remind	tell	wish*
beg	convince	forbid	invite	permit	request*	urge	would like*

* In the active voice, these verbs can be followed by the infinitive without an object (example: *want to speak* or *want someone to speak*).

VERBS THAT CAN BE FOLLOWED BY A GERUND OR AN INFINITIVE

with a change in meaning		without a change in meaning				
forget	remember	begin	continue	like	prefer	try
regret	stop	can't stand	hate	love	start	

ADJECTIVES FOLLOWED BY AN INFINITIVE*

afraid	ashamed	depressed	eager	fortunate	lucky	relieved	surprised
alarmed	certain	determined	easy	glad	pleased	reluctant	touched
amazed	content	disappointed	embarrased	happy	prepared	sad	upset
angry	curious	distressed	encouraged	hesitant	proud	shocked	willing
anxious	delighted	disturbed	excited	likely	ready	sorry	

*Example: *I'm willing **to accept** that.*

PARTICIPIAL ADJECTIVES*

alarming	–	alarmed	embarrassing	–	embarrassed	paralyzing	–	paralyzed
amazing	–	amazed	enlightening	–	enlightened	pleasing	–	pleased
amusing	–	amused	entertaining	–	entertained	relaxing	–	relaxed
annoying	–	annoyed	exciting	–	excited	satisfying	–	satisfied
astonishing	–	astonished	exhausting	–	exhausted	shocking	–	shocked
boring	–	bored	fascinating	–	fascinated	soothing	–	soothed
confusing	–	confused	frightening	–	frightened	startling	–	startled
depressing	–	depressed	horrifying	–	horrified	stimulating	–	stimulated
disappointing	–	disappointed	inspiring	–	inspired	surprising	–	surprised
disgusting	–	disgusted	interesting	–	interested	terrifying	–	terrified
distressing	–	distressed	irritating	–	irritated	tiring	–	tired
disturbing	–	disturbed	moving	–	moved	touching	–	touched

amaze	contain	feel*	look like	please	smell*
appear*	cost	forget	look*	possess	sound
appreciate	desire	hate	love	prefer	suppose
astonish	dislike	have*	matter	realize	surprise
be*	doubt	hear	mean	recognize	taste*
believe	envy	imagine	mind	remember*	think*
belong	equal	include*	need	resemble	understand
care	exist	know	owe	see*	want*
consist of	fear	like	own	seem	weigh*

*These verbs also have action meanings. Example: *I see a tree.* (non-action) *I'm seeing her tomorrow.* (action)

TRANSITIVE PHRASAL VERBS

Some transitive phrasal verbs have more than one meaning. Not all are included here.

Abbreviations
s.o. = someone
sth. = something
e.g. = for example
inf. = informal

SEPARABLE

blow sth. **out**   stop a flame by blowing on it
blow sth. **up**   **1** make sth. explode   **2** fill sth. with air, e.g., a balloon   **3** make sth. larger, e.g., a photo
bring sth. **about**   make sth. happen
bring sth. **back**   **1** return sth. to a store   **2** revive or renew sth., e.g., a custom or tradition
bring sth. **out**   **1** introduce a new product   **2** make a quality more noticeable
bring s.o. **up**   raise a child
bring sth. **up**   start to talk about an issue
burn sth. **down**   burn a structure completely
call s.o. **back**   return a phone call
call sth. **off**   cancel sth.
call s.o. **up**   call s.o. on the phone
carry sth. **out**   conduct a plan
check s.o./sth. **out**   look at s.o. or sth. more closely
cheer s.o. **up**   make s.o. feel happier
clean s.o./sth. **up**   clean s.o. or sth. completely
clear sth. **up**   clarify sth.
close sth. **down**   force a business or institution to close
cover sth. **up**   **1** cover sth. completely   **2** change facts to avoid responsibility
cross sth. **out**   draw a line through sth.
cut sth. **down**   make sth. fall by cutting, e.g., a tree
cut sth. **off**   **1** remove sth. by cutting   **2** stop the supply of sth.
cut s.o. **off**   interrupt s.o who is speaking
dream sth. **up**   invent or think of a new idea
drink sth. **up**   drink a beverage completely
drop s.o./sth. **off**   leave s.o. or sth. somewhere
empty sth. **out**   empty sth. completely
figure s.o./sth. **out**   understand s.o. or sth. after some thought
fill s.o. **in**   tell s.o. about recent events
fill sth. **out**   complete a form
fill sth. **up**   fill a container completely
find sth. **out**   learn new information
follow sth. **through**   do everything to complete a task
get sth. **across**   help s.o. understand an idea
give sth. **away**   give sth. you do not need or want
give sth. **back**   return sth. to its owner
give sth. **out**   distribute sth.
give sth. **up**   quit doing sth.
hand sth. **in**   submit work, e.g., to a boss or a teacher
hand sth. **out**   distribute sth.
hang sth. **up**   put sth. on a hanger or hook, e.g., clothes
help s.o. **out**   assist s.o.
keep s.o./sth. **away**   cause s.o. or sth. to stay at a distance
lay s.o. **off**   fire s.o. because of economic conditions
leave sth. **on**   **1** not turn sth. off, e.g., an appliance   **2** not remove sth. such as clothing or jewelry

leave sth. **out**   omit sth.
let s.o. **down**   disappoint s.o.
let s.o./sth. **in**   allow s.o. or sth. to enter
let s.o. **off**   allow s.o. to leave a bus, car, taxi, etc.
let s.o./sth. **out**   allow s.o. or sth. to leave
light sth. **up**   illuminate sth.
look s.o./sth. **over**   examine s.o. or sth.
look s.o./sth. **up**   **1** try to find s.o.   **2** try to find sth. in a book, the Internet, etc.
make sth. **up**   create a fictional story
pass sth. **out**   distribute sth.
pass sth. **up**   decide not to take an opportunity
pay s.o. **off**   bribe s.o.
pay sth. **off**   pay back money one owes
pick s.o./sth. **out**   identify or choose s.o. or sth.
pick s.o. **up**   stop a vehicle so s.o. can get in
pick s.o./sth. **up**   lift s.o. or sth.
pick sth. **up**   **1** get or buy sth. from somewhere   **2** learn sth. new   **3** get an infectious disease
point s.o./sth. **out**   show s.o or sth. to another person
put sth. **away**   put sth. in its appropriate place
put sth. **back**   return sth. to its original place
put s.o./sth. **down**   **1** stop holding or lifting s.o. or sth.   **2** insult s.o.
put sth. **off**   delay or postpone sth.
put sth. **on**   get dressed or place sth. on one's body
put sth. **together**   **1** put sth. on a wall   **2** build sth.
put sth. **up**   build or erect sth.
set sth. **off**   cause sth. to explode
set sth. **up**   **1** establish a new business, organization, etc.   **2** prepare equipment for use
show s.o./sth. **off**   display the best qualities of s.o. or sth.
shut sth. **off**   stop a machine or supply
straighten sth. **up**   make sth. neat
switch sth. **on**   start a machine, turn on a light, etc.
take sth. **away**   remove sth.
take sth. **back**   **1** return sth. to a store   **2** accept sth. returned by another person
take sth. **down**   remove sth. that is hanging
take sth. **in**   **1** notice and remember sth.   **2** make a clothing item smaller
take sth. **off**   remove clothing, jewelry, etc.
take s.o. **on**   hire s.o.
take sth. **on**   agree to do a task
take s.o. **out**   invite s.o. somewhere and pay for his/her meal, show, etc.
take sth. **up**   start doing an activity habitually
talk sth. **over**   discuss sth.
tear sth. **down**   destroy sth.

tear sth. **up**   tear sth. into small pieces
think sth. **over**   consider sth.
think sth. **up**   invent or think of a new idea
throw sth. **away**   put sth. in the garbage
throw sth. **out**   put sth. in the garbage
touch sth. **up**   improve sth. with very small changes
try sth. **on**   try clothing to see if it fits
try sth. **out**   use sth. to see if one likes it or if it works
turn sth. **around**   **1** turn so the front is at the back **2** cause
                     things to get better
turn s.o./sth. **down**   reject s.o. or sth.
turn sth. **down**   lower the volume, heat, etc.

turn sth. **in**   submit a paper, application, etc.
turn sth. **off**   stop a machine, light, etc.
turn s.o. **off**   cause s.o. to lose interest (inf.)
turn sth. **on**   start a machine, light, etc.
turn sth. **out**   make or manufacture sth.
turn sth. **over**   turn sth. so the bottom is at the top
turn sth. **up**   raise the volume, heat, etc.
use sth. **up**   use sth. completely
wake s.o. **up**   cause s.o. to stop sleeping
wipe sth. **out**   remove or destroy sth.
work sth. **out**   **1** resolve a problem **2** calculate a math problem
write sth. **down**   write sth. to have a record of it

ALWAYS SEPARATED

ask s.o. **over**   invite s.o. to one's home
bring s.o./sth. **down**   remove a ruler or government from power
do sth. **over**   do sth. again
keep sth. **on**   not remove sth. such as clothing or jewelry

see sth. **through**   complete a task
start sth. **over**   begin sth. again
talk s.o. **into** sth.   persuade s.o. to do sth.

INSEPARABLE

cater **to** s.o.   provide what s.o. wants or needs
carry **on** sth.   continue sth. another person has started
come **across** s.o./sth.   find s.o. or sth. unexpectedly
count **on** s.o./sth.   depend on s.o. or sth.
do **without** s.o./sth.   live without s.o. or sth. one needs or wants
go **after** s.o./sth.   pursue s.o. or sth.

go **over** sth.   examine sth. carefully
go **without** sth.   live without sth. one needs or wants
run **into** s.o.   meet s.o. unexpectedly
run **into** sth.   accidentally hit or crash into sth.
stick **with** s.o.   stay close to s.o.
stick **with** sth.   continue doing sth. as before

INTRANSITIVE PHRASAL VERBS

Some intransitive phrasal verbs have more than one meaning. Not all are included here.

blow up   **1** explode **2** suddenly become very angry
break down   stop functioning
break out   start suddenly, e.g., a war, disease, or fire
burn down   burn completely
call back   return a phone call
carry on   **1** continue doing sth. **2** behave in a silly or emotional way
catch on   become popular
check in   report one's arrival at an airport or hotel
check out   pay one's bill and leave a hotel
cheer up   become happier
clear up   become better, e.g., a rash or the weather
close down   stop operating, e.g., a factory or a school
come along   accompany s.o.
come back   return
come in   enter
come off   become unattached
come out   **1** appear, e.g., the sun **2** be removed, e.g., a stain
dress up   wear more formal clothes or a costume
drop in   visit unexpectedly
drop out   quit a class, school, or program
eat out   eat in a restaurant
empty out   empty completely
fall off   become unattached
fill out   become bigger
fill up   become completely full
find out   learn new information
follow through   continue working on sth. until it is completed
fool around   have fun or not be serious
get ahead   make progress or succeed
get along   to not argue
get back   return from a place
get together   meet somewhere with a friend or acquaintance
get up   get out of bed
give up   quit
go along   **1** accompany s.o. **2** agree
go back   return

go off   explode; make a sudden noise
go on   continue to talk about or describe sth.
go out   **1** leave a building **2** leave one's home to meet people,
         enjoy entertainment, etc.
go up   be built
grow up   become an adult
help out   do sth. helpful
hang up   end a phone call
hold on   wait during a phone call
keep away   stay at a distance
keep on   continue
keep up   go or think as fast as another person
lie down   rest on a bed
light up   **1** begin to shine brightly **2** look pleased or happy
make up   end an argument and reestablish a friendly relationship
pass out   become unconscious
pay off   be worthwhile
pick up   improve, e.g., the economy
play around   have fun or not be serious
run out   no longer in supply
show up   appear
sign up   register
sit down   sit
slip up   make a mistake
stand up   rise to one's feet
start over   begin again
stay up   not go to bed
straighten up   make neat
take off   depart by plane
turn in   go to bed (inf.)
turn out   have a particular result
turn up   appear
wake up   stop sleeping
watch out   be careful
work out   **1** exercise **2** be resolved; end successfully

Some three-word phrasal verbs have more than one meaning. Not all are included here.

catch up on sth.   **1** do sth. one didn't have time to do earlier
                  2 get the most recent information
catch up with s.o.   exchange information about recent activities
check up on s.o.   make sure s.o. is OK
come away with sth.   learn sth. useful from s.o. or sth.
come down to sth.   be the most important point or idea
come down with sth.   get an illness
come up against s.o./sth.   be faced with a difficult person or
                       situation
come up with sth.   think of an idea, plan, or solution
face up to sth.   accept an unpleasant truth
fall back on sth.   use an old idea because new ideas have failed
follow through on sth.   continue doing sth. until it is completed
get around to sth.   finally do sth.
get away with sth.   avoid the consequences of a wrong act
get back at s.o.   harm s.o. because he / she harmed you
give up on s.o.   stop hoping that s.o. will change

give up on sth.   stop trying to make sth. happen
go along with sth.   agree to do sth.
go through with sth.   do sth. difficult or painful
grow out of sth.   stop doing sth. as one becomes an adult
keep up with s.o.   stay in regular contact
look down on s.o.   think one is better than another person
look out for s.o.   protect s.o.
look up to s.o.   admire or respect s.o.
make up for sth.   do sth. to apologize
put up with s.o./sth.   accept s.o. or sth. without complaining
run out of sth.   no longer have enough of sth.
stand up for sth.   support an idea or a principle
stand up to s.o.   refuse to let s.o. treat anyone badly
team up with s.o.   do a task together
think back on s.o./sth.   think about and remember s.o. or sth.
walk out on s.o.   end a relationship with a wife, boyfriend, etc.
watch out for s.o./sth.   protect s.o. or sth.

Verb forms: overview

SUMMARY OF VERB FORMS

	Present time	Past time	Future time
Simple	Simple present walk / walks	Simple past walked	Simple future will walk
Continuous	Present continuous am walking / is walking / are walking	Past continuous was walking / were walking	Future continuous will be walking
Perfect	Present perfect have walked / has walked	Past perfect had walked	Future perfect will have walked
Perfect continuous	Present perfect continuous have been walking / has been walking	Past perfect continuous had been walking	Future perfect continuous will have been walking

SIMPLE VERB FORMS: USAGE

	Present time	Past time	Future time
Simple verb forms describe habitual actions or events that occur at a definite time.	Simple present[1] **Habitual action** *The department **meets** once a month to review the status of projects.* **Facts and generalizations** *The Earth **rotates** around the sun every 365 days.*	Simple past **Completed action that occurred at a definite time in the past** *Last year researchers **discovered** a new cancer treatment.* **Habitual action in the past**[2] *When I was young we **visited** my grandparents every week.*	Simple future[3] **Action that will occur at a definite time in the future** *Next year they **will offer** a course on global trade.* **Habitual action in the future** *Next month I'll **go** to the gym three times a week.*

[1] The simple present tense can also express a future action: *Her flight arrives this evening at eight.*

[2] <u>Used to</u> and <u>would</u> also express habitual actions in the past: *When I was a child, we used to spend the summer in the mountains. In the mornings we would go hiking and in the afternoons we would swim in a nearby lake.*

[3] <u>Be going to</u> can also express a future action: *Next year they are going to offer a course on global trade.*

CONTINUOUS VERB FORMS: USAGE

	Present time	Past time	Future time
Continuous verb forms describe continuous actions or events that occur at a definite time.	**Present continuous*** **Action in progress now** *The business managers are discussing next year's budget right now.*	**Past continuous** **Action in progress at a definite time in the past** *None of the computers were working when I came in this morning.*	**Future continuous** **Action that will be in progress during a definite time in the future** *We'll be listening to the speech when you arrive.*

*The present continuous can also express a future plan: *They're getting married next month.*

PERFECT VERB FORMS: USAGE

	Present time	Past time	Future time
Perfect verb forms describe actions or events in relation to other time frames.	**Present perfect*** **Completed action that occurred at an indefinite time before the present** *She has made many contributions to the field.* **Recently completed action** *He has just published an article about his findings.* **Uncompleted action (action that began in the past, continues into the present, and may continue into the future)** *They have studied ancient cultures for many years.*	**Past perfect** **Action that occurred at some point before a definite time in the past** *By 2016, he had started a new business.* **Action that occurred before another past action** *They had already finished medical school when the war broke out.*	**Future perfect** **Action that will be completed by some point at a definite time in the future** *By this time next year, I will have completed my research.*

*Many statements in the present perfect can also be stated correctly using the simple past tense, depending on the speaker's perspective: *She made many contributions to the field.*

PERFECT CONTINUOUS VERB FORMS: USAGE

	Present time	Past time	Future time
Perfect continuous verb forms describe continuous actions or events in relation to other time frames.	**Present perfect continuous** **Uncompleted continuous action (action that began in the past, continues into the present, and may continue into the future)** *She has been lecturing about that topic since 2015.* **Very recently completed action** *The workers have been protesting. They're finished now.*	**Past perfect continuous** **Continuous action that occurred before another past action or time** *By 2015, researchers had been seeking a cure for AIDS for more than thirty years.*	**Future perfect continuous** **Continuous action that occurred before another action or time in the future** *When the new director takes over, I will have been working at this company for ten years.*

SUMMIT 2B

Boosters

Grammar Booster

The Grammar Booster is optional. It provides more explanation and practice, as well as additional related grammar concepts and review.

UNIT 6

The conditional: summary and extension

Type	Use	If clause (states the condition)	Result clause (states the result)	Examples
Factual conditional	To express a general or scientific fact	simple present Note: In this type of conditional, if can be replaced by when or whenever.	simple present	*If it **rains**, the gardens **close** early.* *Water **freezes** if the temperature **falls** below zero degrees Celsius.*
	To talk about what will happen in the future under certain conditions	simple present Note: Don't use a future form in the if clause.	will / be going to + base form of the verb Note: Use can, may, might, should if the result is not certain.	*If you **plan** your trip carefully, things **will go** smoothly.* *If we **arrive** late, they're **going to start** without us.* *If we **hurry**, we **may be able to catch** the train.*
Present unreal conditional	To talk about present unreal or untrue conditions	simple past or were Note: Don't use would in the if clause.	would + base form of the verb Note: Use could or might if the result is not certain.	*If I **had** the time, I **would explain** the problem to you.* *If he **were** here, he **might make** a lot of changes.*
Past unreal conditional	To talk about past unreal or untrue conditions	past perfect Note: Don't use would have in the if clause.	would have + past participle Note: Use could have or might have if the result is not certain.	*If they **had known** about the storm, they **would have taken** a different flight.* *If you **had told** us about the delay, we **could have made** other arrangements.*
Mixed time frames	To talk about past unreal or untrue conditions in relation to the present	past perfect Note: Don't use would in the if clause.	would + base form of the verb Note: Use could or might if the result is not certain.	*If I **had prepared** for the interview, I **wouldn't be** so nervous.* *If we **had left** earlier, we **might be** on time now.*
	To talk about present unreal or untrue conditions in relation to the past	simple past or were Note: Don't use would have in the if clause.	would have + past participle Note: Use could have or might have if the result is not certain.	*If she **were** honest, she **would have told** us the truth.* *If I **spoke** Russian, I **might have understood** the guide.*

Extension: other uses

Use should, happen to, or should happen to in the if clause in factual conditionals when the condition is less likely.

If you {
should
happen to
should happen to
} see Peter, tell him to call me.

To express inferences in conditional sentences, different combinations of tenses can be used.

If Julie **went** to the party last night, she definitely **saw** what happened.

If you **don't know** the answer to this question, you **didn't do** your homework.

If the results **didn't come out** yesterday, they'll definitely **come out** today.

If you still **haven't finished** packing by now, you're **not going to catch** your flight.

A Circle the correct word or words to complete each sentence.

1 If Sam (does / will do) well this year, he will apply to medical school.

2 Water (boils / is going to boil) when the temperature reaches 100 degrees Celsius.

3 If you (will / should) find my scarf, please hold it for me.

4 If you (happen / happen to) see a good camera at the market, please buy it for me.

5 If it (wouldn't have been / hadn't been) for her savings, Anna wouldn't have been able to attend university.

6 If we (would have known / had known) that car insurance was so expensive, we would not have bought a car.

7 If you didn't get a reply today, you (would definitely hear / will definitely hear) from us tomorrow.

8 If I (had / would have) a garden, I would grow several types of flowers.

9 If I (would have practiced / had practiced) my speech a bit more, I might not be so worried now.

10 If I (should happen to / will) see John, I'll tell him to call you.

UNIT 7

Article usage: summary

Note where indefinite or definite articles are used or omitted.

	Indefinite article	Definite article	No article
General statement	Use with singular count nouns: **A cat** *may symbolize good fortune.*	Use with singular count nouns: **The cat** *may symbolize good fortune.* Use with non-count nouns: *Freud called attention to* **the importance** *of dreams.*	With plural count nouns: **Cats** *may symbolize good fortune.* With non-count nouns: **Misfortune** *may strike at any time.*
First mention	Use with singular count nouns: *I found* **a** *lucky charm.*		With plural count nouns: *I have (some) lucky* **charms**. With non-count nouns: *I bought (some)* **shampoo**.
Second mention		Use with singular count nouns: **The** *lucky* **charm** *was in a box.* Use with plural count nouns: **The** *lucky* **charms** *were in a box.* Use with non-count nouns: **The shampoo** *is in the closet.*	

A On a separate sheet of paper, rewrite the paragraph, correcting eleven errors and making any necessary changes.

The homes are expensive these days, but Peter got lucky and bought small house last week. A house has two bedrooms and one bathroom. It also has large kitchen and the living room. Peter will use a living room as his home office. Bedrooms are in bad condition, and Peter will need a help painting them. Then he wants to have the party so his friends can admire a house. Later Peter will buy a furniture—when he saves some money!

Definite article: additional uses

When a noun represents a unique thing	Use with singular count nouns: **The sun** *rises in the east.*
With a comparative or superlative adjective to make a noun unique (or with <u>right</u>, <u>wrong</u>, <u>first</u>, <u>only</u>, <u>same</u>)	Use with singular count nouns: *Telling the truth is* **the best course** *of action. It's always* **the right thing** *to do.* *The robin is* **the first sign** *of spring.* Use with plural count nouns: *People in different places often have* **the same superstitions**. Use with non-count nouns: *That's* **the only information** *I was able to find on the Internet.*

When context makes a noun specific	Use with singular count nouns:
	    The hospital in this town has an excellent emergency room.
	Use with plural count nouns:
	    The buildings in this town are no higher than ten stories.
	Use with non-count nouns:
	    The air in this city is polluted.

When an adjective clause makes a noun specific	Use with singular count nouns:
	    The mirror that you broke will bring you bad luck.
	Use with plural count nouns:
	    The mirrors that you broke will bring you bad luck.
	Use with non-count nouns:
	    The progress that she made was due not to good luck but to hard work.

When an adjective represents a certain group of people	Use with a noun derived from an adjective, such as the blind, the deaf, the dead, the living, the young, the old, the poor, the rich, the unemployed, the privileged, the underprivileged: *The unemployed* must often learn new job skills.

B Complete the paragraphs with words from the box. Use a definite article when appropriate.

tourists	gasoline	view	world	wealthy	sky	ballooning	first men

On March 20, 1999, Bertrand Piccard of Switzerland and Brian Jones of Britain were ....

1

to travel around .... in a balloon. The numerous balloonists who had been attempting this

2

journey for decades beforehand ran into various problems with weather and equipment.

In the past several years, ... has become a popular adventure sport. Due to the high cost of balloons

3

and .... , however, it is a sport reserved for .... can get a taste of ballooning during

4   5   6

their travels. .... of a city or landscape from .... is always breathtaking.

7   8

More non-count nouns with both a countable and an uncountable sense

With some non-count nouns, the change in meaning is subtle: The countable meaning refers to something specific and the uncountable meaning refers to something general.

a fear = the anticipation of a specific danger; a phobia
    He had **a fear** of heights.
	fear = a general anticipation of danger
	    Irrational **fear** can lead to anxiety.

a victory = a specific event in which mastery or success is achieved
    The battle of Waterloo was **a** great **victory** for the English.
	victory = the phenomenon of winning
	    She led her party to **victory**.

a time = a specific moment in the past or future; a specific occasion
    There was **a time** when food was much cheaper.
    How **many times** did you read it?
	time = the general concept; clock time
	    Time passes so quickly!
	    What **time** did you arrange to meet?

a superstition = a specific belief or practice
    A common **superstition** is that a black cat brings bad luck.
	superstition = a general attitude
	    The prevalence of **superstition** today is surprising.

C Write <u>a</u> before a noun where necessary. Write <u>X</u> if a noun should not have an article.

1 a Will people ever learn to control their phobias? Only .... time can tell.

  b There has never been .... time when people didn't try to interpret their dreams.

2 a If you have .... fear of flying, you shouldn't take a job that requires overseas travel.

  b Psychologists agree that .... fear is a universal emotion.

3 a Ignorance and fear may sometimes lead to .... superstition.

   b There is .... widely held superstition that knocking on wood brings good luck.

4 a The coach's tactics helped the team win .... major victory in last night's game.

   b Everyone cannot always experience the joy of .... victory; someone has to lose.

Grammar for Writing: indirect speech with passive reporting verbs

A passive reporting verb can be followed by an infinitive phrase.

   Most superstitions are believed **to be** false.

The infinitive phrase reflects the time of the reporting verb. It can be simple, continuous, perfect, or perfect continuous.

   This book is said **to be** excellent.

   The robber was reported **to be running away** from the scene of the crime.

   The car is believed **never to have been** in an accident before.

   She was thought **to have been preparing** dinner when she got sick.

D On a separate sheet of paper, change each of the following sentences from the active voice to the passive voice.

   1 Many people believe that flying isn't as safe as driving.

   2 They reported the driver was talking on his phone when he crashed into the back of that van.

   3 Everyone says the tour was overpriced, but others think the price was very fair.

   4 People have said the article was a lie, but it turned out to be perfectly true.

UNIT 8

Grammar for Writing: emphatic stress

In informal writing, you can underline the verb <u>be</u>, a modal, or an auxiliary verb to indicate emphatic stress.
The addition of <u>do</u> for emphatic stress does not require underlining. In more formal writing, with the exception of adding the auxiliary <u>do</u>, emphatic stress is avoided.

   She <u>is</u> good at math, isn't she?

   Even though it was getting late, I <u>would</u> have liked to stay longer.

   I suddenly realized that I <u>had</u> been there before.

   BUT She didn't answer her phone, but she did text me.

> In the modal-like expression <u>had better</u>, underline <u>better</u>, not <u>had</u>.
> He'd <u>better</u> pay attention in class!

A Use the prompts to write B's response with emphatic stress. Add the auxiliary <u>do</u> if possible, and underline stressed verb <u>be</u>, modal, or other auxiliary verb.

   1 A: Do you worry much about global warming?

   B: .... (I think about it) from time to time.

   2 A: Would you say you have a way with words?

   B: .... (I express myself) clearly.

   3 A: I'm thinking of applying to medical school, but I haven't made up my mind yet.

   B: Well, ... (you should apply).

   4 A: Do you have to pass any kind of tests to get a job at the Mason Corporation?

   B: .... (you have to take) an EQ test.

   5 A: Shouldn't Jamie hurry if she wants to catch the 3:00 bus?

   B: .... (She'd better hurry). That's the last bus.

   6 A: Would you like me to introduce you to my brother?

   B: .... (I'd like to meet) him.

   7 A: Would you like to grab dinner somewhere together?

   B: .... (I've already had) dinner.

Infinitives and gerunds in place of the subjunctive

Certain statements in the subjunctive can be rephrased less formally by changing <u>that</u> to <u>for</u> and using an infinitive.

It is essential **for** John **to find** the time each day to relax. (= It is essential that John **find** the time each day to relax.)

An infinitive can also be used without a <u>for</u> phrase. It usually refers to "people in general."

It is essential **to find** the time each day to relax.

Certain statements in the subjunctive can be rephrased using a gerund if it refers to "people in general."

Dr. Sharpe recommends **spending** a few moments relaxing. (= Dr. Sharpe recommends that people **spend** a few moments relaxing.)

B Rewrite each sentence less formally, using infinitives and gerunds. Make any necessary changes.

1 It is crucial that you practice feng shui.

2 The article suggests that you carry lucky charms.

3 The manager recommended that they finish the project fast.

4 It is important that we get enough sleep every night.

5 The directions advise that you add salt.

6 It is necessary that she arrive at the theater by 4:00 P.M.

UNIT 9

Grammar for Writing: when to use the passive voice

Passive sentences focus attention on the result of an action rather than on the performer (agent) of the action. Writers prefer the passive voice in the following situations:

1 To emphasize the result of an action, or if the agent is unimportant or unknown. This use is common in academic writing, scientific articles, and news reports.

Some sophisticated treatments **have been developed**. (emphasizes the treatments, not the people who developed them)

Hundreds of people **were made** homeless by yesterday's floods. (emphasizes the result, not the floods themselves)

2 To describe a process. This use is found in technical and scientific writing.

There are four basic steps in the commercial production of orange juice. First the oranges **are unloaded** from trucks and **placed** on a conveyor belt. Then they **are washed** and **sorted**. Next they **are put** into machines that remove the juice and put it into cartons.

3 To use an impersonal or indirect tone, which suggests formality, impartiality, or objectivity. This use is favored in official documents, formal announcements, and signs, or to avoid placing blame.

Walking on the grass **is prohibited**.

An error **has been made** in your account. It **will be corrected** on next month's statement. (The writer avoids mentioning who made the mistake and emphasizes the fact that it will be corrected, rather than who will do the correcting.)

4 To keep the reader's attention focused on a previously mentioned noun, because it is the central topic of the paragraph.

They caught the thief later that evening. He **was placed** in jail and **was allowed** to call a lawyer. (The topic is the thief. By using the passive voice in the second sentence, the writer keeps the reader's attention focused on the thief.)

5 To avoid using a "general subject." General subjects include the impersonal <u>you</u>, <u>we</u>, and <u>they</u>; <u>people</u>; <u>one</u>; <u>someone</u> / <u>somebody</u>; <u>anyone</u> / <u>anybody</u>. This use is common in formal documents, in official signs, and in newspaper editorials and other texts that express an opinion.

People must show their IDs before boarding. PREFERRED: IDs **must be shown** before boarding.

Someone should inform consumers of their rights. PREFERRED: Consumers **should be informed** of their rights.

6 To avoid awkward sentence constructions. This is a common solution when the agent has a long or complex modifier.

The Tigers, whose new strategy of offense and defense seemed to be working, defeated the Lions.

PREFERRED: The Lions **were defeated** by the Tigers, whose new strategy of offense and defense seemed to be working.

A On a separate sheet of paper, write each sentence in the passive voice.

1 Construction workers built the museum in less than six months.

2 People must present their passports at the border.

3 First, engineers perfect the design for the new product. Then, workers build a prototype. Next, engineers test the prototype. After engineers approve the design, the factory begins production.

4 We have credited the sum of eighty-five dollars to your VISTA account.

5 The reporter, whose investigation uncovered many shocking facts and a pattern of corrupt behavior, exposed the official for taking bribes.

Phrasal verbs: expansion

The passive form of phrasal verbs

Transitive phrasal verbs are always inseparable in the passive voice, even when they are separable or always separated in the active voice.

I couldn't **turn on** the TV (OR **turn** the TV **on**). → The TV couldn't be **turned on**.

They **turned** the empty lot **into** a beautiful → The empty lot was **turned into** garden. a beautiful garden.

> **Remember**
> Intransitive phrasal verbs are always inseparable. They can't be used in the passive voice since they don't have direct objects.

Transitive and intransitive meanings

Some phrasal verbs have both a transitive and an intransitive meaning.

He went to bed without **taking off** his clothes. (transitive meaning: remove)

What time does your plane **take off**? (intransitive meaning: leave)

She **broke in** the new employees by showing them the procedures. (transitive meaning: train someone)

Thieves **broke in** and stole her jewelry. (intransitive meaning: enter by force)

For a complete list of transitive and intransitive phrasal verbs, see the Reference Charts, pages 124–125.

Three-word phrasal verbs

A three-word phrasal verb consists of a verb, a particle, and a preposition that together have a specific meaning. The verb, the particle, and the preposition in three-word phrasal verbs are inseparable.

As a result of his controversial ideas, the senator **came up against** members of his own party, who opposed him vigorously.

Does society have an obligation to **look out for** people who are disadvantaged?

Temper tantrums are not uncommon in young children. As they mature, they **grow out of** this behavior.

I'm going to close my door and not take any calls today; I've just got to **catch up on** my work.

For a complete list of three-word phrasal verbs, see the Reference Charts, page 126.

A On a separate sheet of paper, rewrite each sentence in the passive voice. Do not include a <u>by</u> phrase.

1 We have to call the meeting off.
2 He talked the client into a better deal.
3 They covered the mistake up.
4 She dropped the children off in front of the school.
5 One of the applicants filled the form out incorrectly.
6 I paid the balance off last month.
7 Someone threw the document away.
8 The speaker handed pamphlets out at the end of the presentation.

B Underline the phrasal verb in each sentence. Then decide if it has a transitive or an intransitive meaning.

transitive   intransitive

1 ☐ ☐ The photographer blew up the photo 200 percent so we could use it for the poster.
2 ☐ ☐ The plane blew up shortly before it was supposed to land.
3 ☐ ☐ The workers won't give up until they're paid fair wages.
4 ☐ ☐ She has tried to give up smoking several times, without success.
5 ☐ ☐ Phil has to wake up at 5:00 A.M. every morning to get to work on time.
6 ☐ ☐ The children played quietly in order not to wake up their parents.
7 ☐ ☐ He works out three or four times a week in order to stay healthy.
8 ☐ ☐ World leaders are meeting to work out a plan to eradicate poverty.

Pronunciation Booster

The Pronunciation Booster is optional. It provides a pronunciation lesson and practice to support speaking in each unit, making students' speech more comprehensible.

UNIT 6

Regular past participle endings

There are three pronunciations of the past participle ending -ed, depending on the final sound of the base form of the verb.

With voiced sounds (except /d/)
When the base form ends with a voiced sound, pronounce the -ed ending as /d/.

moved   canceled   described   stayed   agreed

With voiceless sounds (except /t/)
When the base form ends with a voiceless sound, pronounce the -ed ending as /t/.

helped   asked   crushed   watched

HOWEVER: When the base form ends with the sound /t/ or /d/, pronounce the -ed ending as a new syllable, /ɪd/ or /əd/. In American English, the final sound before the -ed ending is always /t̪/, no matter whether the base form ended in the sound /t/ or /d/. Link /t̪/ with the -ed ending.

wai ted	→	/weit̪ɪd/	nee ded	→	/nit̪ɪd/
re por ted	→	/rɪpɔrt̪ɪd/	in clud ed	→	/ɪnklut̪ɪd/

Voiced sounds		Voiceless sounds
/b/	/i/	/p/
/g/	/ɪ/	/k/
/ð/	/eɪ/	/θ/
/v/	/ɛ/	/f/
/z/	/æ/	/s/
/ʒ/	/ɑ/	/ʃ/
/dʒ/	/ɔ/	/tʃ/
/m/	/oʊ/	/t/
/n/	/ʊ/	
/ŋ/	/u/	
/r/	/ʌ/	
/l/	/d/	

Reduction in perfect modals

The auxiliary have in perfect modals is generally reduced. The /h/ is dropped and /æ/ is reduced to /ə/.

/wʊt̪əv/
If I'd looked at the expiration date, I **would have** renewed my passport.

/maɪt̪əv/
If I weren't Japanese, I **might have** needed a visa to enter the country.

/wʊt̪ənəv/
If we'd left on time, we **wouldn't have** missed our flight.

Perfect modals

would have ⎫
could have ⎪
should have ⎬ + [past participle]
might have ⎪
may have ⎭

A ▶6:14 Listen and practice.

1 moved	**5** agreed	**9** watched	**12** needed
2 canceled	**6** helped	**10** waited	**13** included
3 described	**7** asked	**11** reported	
4 stayed	**8** crushed		

B ▶6:15 Listen and practice.

1 If I'd looked at the expiration date, I would have renewed my passport.

2 If I weren't Japanese, I might have needed a visa to enter the country.

3 If we'd left on time, we wouldn't have missed our flight.

C Circle the correct pronunciation of each -ed ending.

1 avoided	/ɪd/	/t/	/d/	**9** promised	/ɪd/	/t/	/d/
2 looked	/ɪd/	/t/	/d/	**10** covered	/ɪd/	/t/	/d/
3 summarized	/ɪd/	/t/	/d/	**11** added	/ɪd/	/t/	/d/
4 arrived	/ɪd/	/t/	/d/	**12** changed	/ɪd/	/t/	/d/
5 owed	/ɪd/	/t/	/d/	**13** reported	/ɪd/	/t/	/d/
6 ruined	/ɪd/	/t/	/d/	**14** discussed	/ɪd/	/t/	/d/
7 kicked	/ɪd/	/t/	/d/	**15** investigated	/ɪd/	/t/	/d/
8 refunded	/ɪd/	/t/	/d/	**16** enjoyed	/ɪd/	/t/	/d/

▶6:16 **Now practice saying each word aloud and listen to compare.***

D ▶6:17 **Practice saying each sentence aloud, paying attention to reductions. Listen to compare.***

1 If I'd put my passport in my briefcase, it wouldn't have gotten lost.

2 If you'd checked the luggage limits, you might have avoided extra charges.

3 If my friend's luggage hadn't gotten stolen, he could have gone on the sightseeing tour.

4 I probably wouldn't have missed my flight if I had come on time.

5 If they'd taken a few simple precautions, their luggage might not have gotten stolen.

UNIT 7

Linking sounds

Link plural noun endings to the first sound in the word that follows.

Superstitions about animals are very common. /supər'stɪʃənzəbout/

Some say rats leaving a ship will cause it to sink. /ræt'slivɪŋ/

Link third-person singular endings to the first sound in the word that follows.

A belief in a superstition often results in fear. /rɪ'zʌltsɪn/

> **Remember:** There are three different sounds for the endings of plural nouns and third-person singular verbs.
>
> | /z/ | /s/ | /ɪz/ |
> |---|---|---|
> | diamonds | results | promises |
> | superstitions | sharks | noises |
> | bottles | types | matches |
> | believes | beliefs | wishes |
> | dreams | sleeps | judges |

A ▶6:18 **Listen and practice.**

1 Superstitions about animals are very common.

2 Some say rats leaving a ship will cause it to sink.

3 A belief in a superstition often results in fear.

B ▶6:19 **Practice reading each sentence aloud, paying attention to the linking sounds you have learned. Listen to compare.*** (Note that your choices may differ from what you hear on the audio.)

1 A frog brings good luck to the house it enters.

2 Babies born with teeth become extremely selfish.

3 An itchy nose means you'll have a fight.

4 A lucky charm protects against the evil eye.

5 She keeps a large bowl of water near the front door.

6 Superstitions can be found in every culture.

7 A company claims to have invented a machine that allows people to talk with their pets.

8 Some fears are hard to overcome.

9 My sister believes in ghosts, avoids black cats, and carries a lucky charm in her pocket.

UNIT 8

Emphatic stress with auxiliary verbs

Use emphatic stress on an auxiliary verb to confirm or contradict.

A: Do you think Carrie Mulligan has a successful acting career?
B: I think so. She **IS** getting a lot of lead roles these days.

A: I wonder if I should take French lessons.
B: Great idea! I think you **SHOULD** learn French.

A: Have you eaten at the Blue Moon Café before?
B: Actually, I think I **HAVE** eaten there before.

A: Jan says you love coffee. Is that true?
B: Not at all. I really **DON'T** like coffee.

Remember: The auxiliary <u>do</u> needs to be added for emphatic stress in affirmative statements in the simple present or past tense.

A: Jan says you love coffee. Is that true?
B: Yes, it is. I really **DO** like coffee.

A ▶6:20 **Listen and practice.**

1 She **IS** getting a lot of lead roles these days.

2 I think you **SHOULD** learn French.

3 Actually, I think I **HAVE** eaten there before.

4 I really **DON'T** like coffee.

5 I really **DO** like coffee.

B ▶6:21 Practice responding to each speaker, using emphatic stress on the auxiliary verb. Listen to compare.*

1 "I think Olivia's a great cook."

RESPONSE: I agree. She does make great food.

2 "Your husband doesn't dance very well."

RESPONSE: That's true. He really doesn't dance well.

3 "Can you eat seafood?"

RESPONSE: Actually, I can't eat seafood. I'm allergic to it.

4 "Your cousins are hysterical!"

RESPONSE: I agree. They really do tell a lot of funny jokes.

5 "Ana's report is late again."

RESPONSE: Well, she does tend to procrastinate.

6 "Does Gary have a head for figures?"

RESPONSE: No. But he is taking a math class on Tuesday evenings.

7 "I think it's time to tell everyone you're going to quit."

RESPONSE: You're right. I should tell them sooner rather than later.

8 "Have you made up your mind yet? "

RESPONSE: No. But I have been thinking about it.

UNIT 9

Reading aloud

Because it's more difficult to understand language when it is read rather than spoken in conversation, read with a regular rhythm and use fewer sound reductions. If there's a title, state it separately with falling intonation. Pause at all punctuation. Separate sentences into thought groups, pausing after each. Pause slightly longer between sentences.

Envisioning the Future
In the 1960s, / only large institutions, / such as banks, / corporations, / and the military, / had computers. // They were expensive, / slow, / and very large— / requiring a special air-conditioned room— / and access to them was limited / to only a few people. // In the 1970s, / computer prices came down / and then small businesses began to use them. // Nevertheless, / in 1977, / the CEO and founder of Digital Equipment, / Kenneth Olsen, / predicted that computers would never be used in the home.

A ▶6:22 Listen to the selection. Then practice reading it aloud.

Envisioning the Future
In the 1960s, only large institutions, such as banks, corporations, and the military, had computers. They were expensive, slow, and very large—requiring a special air-conditioned room—and access to them was limited to only a few people. In the 1970s, computer prices came down and then small businesses began to use them. Nevertheless, in 1977, the CEO and founder of Digital Equipment, Kenneth Olsen, predicted that computers would never be used in the home.

B ▶6:23 Practice reading each selection aloud. Then listen to compare.* (Note that your choices may differ from what you hear on the audio.)

1 **Birth of the Personal Computer**

In the early 80s, Steve Jobs and Bill Gates introduced the personal computer—the Macintosh and the IBM PC, respectively—which made computing at home possible. In 1983, Jobs gave a speech about the future, in which he predicted that, for most people, a great deal of time would be spent interacting with personal computers. He also predicted that, within ten years, computers in the office and at home would be connected so people would be able to use them to communicate.

2 **Predicting Social Media**

In 1999, Gates predicted that small devices would be carried around by everyone so that they could get instant information and stay in touch with others. He also claimed that, by the early twenty-first century, Internet communities would have been formed, based on one's interests or to connect with friends and family.

Intonation of tag questions

When a tag question follows a statement to which a speaker anticipates agreement, both the statement and the tag question are said with falling intonation. The main stress in the tag question falls on the auxiliary verb and not on the pronoun. Note that there is generally no pause at the comma.

It's really shocking, isn't it?

It's not really surprising, is it?

It really makes you feel angry, doesn't it?

They'll come up with a solution, won't they?

She didn't speak out against that project, did she?

When the tag question represents a genuine question to which the speaker expects an answer, the statement is said with falling intonation, but the tag question is said with rising intonation.

It's really shocking, isn't it?

It's not really surprising, is it?

It really makes you feel angry, doesn't it?

They'll come up with a solution, won't they?

She didn't speak out against that project, did she?

A ▶6:24 **Listen and practice. (Each sentence is said two ways.)**

1 It's really shocking, isn't it?

2 It's not really surprising, is it?

3 It really makes you feel angry, doesn't it?

4 They'll come up with a solution, won't they?

5 She didn't speak out against that project, did she?

B ▶6:25 **Listen to the following tag questions. Check to indicate if each one anticipates agreement or expects an answer.**

	Anticipates agreement	Expects an answer
1 That's really appalling, isn't it?	☐	☐
2 He's worried about his children, isn't he?	☐	☐
3 It really makes you feel good, doesn't it?	☐	☐
4 It wasn't really true, was it?	☐	☐
5 They're going to do something about that problem, aren't they?	☐	☐
6 It's not really important, is it?	☐	☐
7 You heard that on TV, didn't you?	☐	☐
8 You'll support us, won't you?	☐	☐

▶6:25 **Now practice saying each tag question aloud and listen to compare.***

C ▶6:26 **Practice saying each tag question two ways, first to express anticipated agreement and then to express a genuine question. Listen to compare.***

1 It really makes you stop and think, doesn't it?

2 They're concerned about global warming, aren't they?

3 The president's economic policy is effective, isn't it?

4 The benefits of globalization are very clear, aren't they?

5 The benefits of globalization aren't very clear, are they?

6 There's no turning back, is there?

Test-Taking Skills Booster

The Test-Taking Skills Booster is optional. It provides practice in applying some key logical thinking and comprehension skills typically included in reading and listening tasks on standardized proficiency tests. Each unit contains one Reading Completion activity and one or more Listening Completion activities.

*Note that the practice activities in the Booster are not intended to test student achievement after each unit. Complete Achievement Tests for **Summit** can be found in the **Summit** ActiveTeach.

UNIT 6

READING COMPLETION

Read the selection. Choose the word or phrase that best completes each statement.

Wi-Fi Safety

Staying connected anywhere is relatively easy today. We almost always have smartphones, tablets, or laptops at the ready. And **(1)** ..... the availability of free Wi-Fi everywhere—in hotels, cafés, stores, even in parks—we feel empowered to act as we do at home. For instance, we can do our online banking and make online purchases anywhere with **(2)** ..... . On the one hand, easy connectivity is a great **(3)** ..... . But on the other, wishful thinking can lull us into a false sense of **(4)** ..... . It's important to remember that **(5)** ..... at home, where our Internet connections are securely encrypted, free public Wi-Fi away from home is not.

What are some of the possible **(6)** ..... of using unencrypted Wi-Fi? First, a thief might be able to access your credit card information and make online or in-store purchases, leaving you to pay the bill. Many such purchases, however, especially if they don't conform to your usual buying pattern, **(7)** ..... the credit card company that the purchaser isn't you. Luckily, the company can cancel your card to stop any further **(8)** ..... from being made. **(9)** ..... , but perhaps more importantly, thieves can **(10)** ..... your usernames and passwords, enabling them to access your bank accounts and withdraw money. Finally, in the worst-case scenario, they can steal your identity, leaving you to **(11)** ..... it at great trouble to you. So how can you **(12)** ..... yourself? In summary, although free public Wi-Fi seems convenient, send personal information only to sites that are fully encrypted, and avoid using any mobile apps that **(13)** ..... personal or financial information.

	A	B	C	D
1	in spite of	since	in addition to	due to
2	aggravation	difficulty	cash	ease
3	advantage	disadvantage	importance	problem
4	disadvantage	the future	security	anxiety
5	like	similarly	unlike	as well
6	reasons	consequences	points of view	possibilities
7	indicate	avoid	alert	accuse
8	purchases	decisions	claims	conflicts
9	Secondly	By the same token	After	Before
10	provide	recover	return	steal
11	recover	relate	return	resist
12	affect	promote	remove	protect
13	provide	require	resist	donate

LISTENING COMPLETION

▶ 6:33 **You will hear part of a report. Read the paragraph below. Then listen and complete each statement with the word or short phrase you hear in the report. Listen a second time to check your work.**

Consider this situation: You are waiting patiently for your bags at (1) .... You see other travelers pick up their bags, but still yours are nowhere in sight. There are fewer and fewer bags until finally (2) .... You wonder what happened to your bags and think perhaps they weren't transferred to your (3) .... when you changed planes. Or maybe the missing luggage was sent to (4) .... You go to the airline's (5) .... to file a claim and hope the bags will (6) .... and be delivered to (7) .... within a short time. If, on the other hand, the bags are permanently (8) .... or completely (9) .... , you will want to file a claim for damages. If you can document what you have lost, you will probably be reimbursed. But be aware that even if you have (10) .... to prove the value of items in your luggage, you won't receive (11) .... you originally paid for your property. But you will definitely receive something.

READING COMPLETION

Read the selection. Choose the word or phrase that best completes each statement.

Coping with Phobias

According to recent research, one in ten people worldwide has some kind of phobia or overwhelming **(1)** ..... . And even though phobias are **(2)** ..... , they are much more severe than the common garden-variety fear. But in what way?

For one thing, while most people can **(3)** ..... with most normal fears, a full-blown phobia is something people can't just put out of their mind. **(4)** ..... , phobics don't have much control over their phobias. As a result, they suffer from unpleasant physical and mental **(5)** ..... when confronted with what they fear. Such symptoms are similar to ones people experience when faced with real physical **(6)** ..... . **(7)** ..... , their heartbeat gets rapid, their throat goes dry, and their sweating increases. These unpleasant physical symptoms are intended to prepare people to **(8)** ..... harm in the face of real danger. However, the phobic, who isn't in any real physical danger, reacts in the same way. **(9)** ..... , phobics will go to great lengths to avoid what they fear and these extremely unpleasant physical responses. **(10)** ..... , there is hope for people with phobias despite their severity. In "cognitive behavioral therapy," or CBT, phobics are repeatedly **(11)** ..... to what causes the fear, which desensitizes them to it because nothing bad happens. If CBT doesn't work, "counter-conditioning" can teach patients to substitute a physical relaxation response when in the presence of what **(12)** ..... them. In summary, there is hope for phobics who get **(13)** ..... . The success rate of therapy is excellent.

1	**A** danger	**B** anxiety	**C** relaxation	**D** need
2	**A** talents	**B** harmful	**C** fears	**D** certain
3	**A** appreciate	**B** come down	**C** cope	**D** notice
4	**A** Fortunately	**B** In other words	**C** Similarly	**D** Even so
5	**A** symptoms	**B** fears	**C** benefits	**D** emotions
6	**A** relief	**B** pleasure	**C** danger	**D** symptoms
7	**A** Even so	**B** For example	**C** However	**D** Moreover
8	**A** undergo	**B** avoid	**C** cause	**D** receive
9	**A** However	**B** Because	**C** In contrast	**D** Consequently
10	**A** For example	**B** While	**C** Unfortunately	**D** Fortunately
11	**A** exposed	**B** allowed	**C** reduced	**D** increased
12	**A** relaxes	**B** helps	**C** angers	**D** frightens
13	**A** success	**B** failure	**C** treatment	**D** ready

LISTENING COMPLETION

A ▶ 6:34 You will hear a conversation. Read the paragraph below. Then listen and complete each statement with the word or short phrase you hear in the conversation. Listen a second time to check your work.

The man is reading about a way (1) .... in a short time. But the woman is doubtful and says it sounds (2) .... He disagrees and explains the scheme: You get a list of (3) .... and then send (4) .... to the last person on the list. Then you add (5) .... to the list. When someone else gets that list, the money (6) .... rolling in. The woman says that this is such an (7) .... get-rich-quick scam.

B ▶ 6:35 You will hear a conversation. Read the paragraph below. Then listen and complete each statement with a word or short phrase you hear in the conversation. Listen a second time to check your work.

The woman says there's a company that has (8) .... for people to learn to speak a new language during the time when they're (9) .... She thinks it's absolutely (10) .... The man, on the other hand, says he wouldn't (11) .... that it's impossible. He says he heard that some (12) .... in a sleep-learning lab had (13) .... the basics of Russian in only one week.

READING COMPLETION

Read the selection. Choose the word or phrase that best completes each statement.

Can We Increase Our Intelligence?

In a general sense, intelligence can be defined as the ability to learn, understand, and apply knowledge or skills. While many experts have argued that one's IQ score simply cannot be **(1)** ..... , others claim that these abilities can be maximized by exercising the brain. In their opinion, certain activities, **(2)** ..... reading regularly, doing puzzles daily, or learning a new language, may in fact improve our thinking skills, capacity to remember, and general knowledge. Furthermore, they make the point that IQ tests don't provide an adequate **(3)** ..... of real intelligence. In fact, they measure how one's level of academic achievement can be predicted but do not measure creativity or "street smarts"—the ability to **(4)** ..... with everyday life. Likewise, they are **(5)** ..... to measure one's potential for growth. Some experts suggest that other aspects of intelligence be considered as well— emotional intelligence being one example.

Moreover, Harvard University's Howard Gardner proposed that psychologists and educators **(6)** ..... the existence of at least seven distinct areas of intelligence. Two of these, linguistic and mathematical, are currently measured to some degrees by IQ tests. **(7)** ..... , another two, interpersonal and intrapersonal, are measured by EQ tests. He also proposed including visual-spatial intelligence. In addition, Gardner recommended that two other aspects of intelligence be **(8)** ..... : musical and physical. Gardner considers each of these intelligences to be areas of human potential; **(9)** ..... , they can be developed and increased.

	A	B	C	D
1	believed	increased	provided	genetic
2	such as	from	for instance	to
3	tool	measurement	improvement	completion
4	measure	encounter	face	deal
5	unable	equipped	incomplete	designed
6	contribute	criticize	acknowledge	change
7	Similarly	As a result	Because of this	For instance
8	recognized	removed	presented	altered
9	otherwise	that is	even so	besides

LISTENING COMPLETION

▶ 6:36 **You will hear part of a lecture. Read the paragraph below. Then listen and complete each statement with the word or short phrase you hear in the lecture. Listen a second time to check your work.**

The lecturer says that a key argument in favor of (1) .... being the source of extreme intelligence is that most geniuses don't have extremely (2) .... ancestors. However, an argument in favor of the (3) .... view is that talented families do (4) .... They believe it shows that talent is (5) .... through genes. One living example that supports this (6) .... is the story of the (7) .... Srinivasa Ramanujan, who was raised in a (8) .... in India and had almost (9) .... in mathematics. In other words, he was (10) .... talent.

READING COMPLETION

Read the selection. Choose the word or phrase that best completes each statement.

Protecting Wildlife and People's Livelihoods

Due to its **(1)** ..... rising population as well as unregulated development, Cambodia's wildlife habitats have been at risk. **(2)** ..... more and more poor, uneducated, and inexperienced farmers have taken up agriculture near the edges of Cambodia's shrinking forests, conflicts with Cambodia's wild Asian elephants have increased. An increasing number of hungry elephants have been searching for food near the edges of the forests. As a consequence, they have **(3)** ..... crops severely, forcing the farmers to kill the elephants in order to protect their livelihoods.

Tuy Sereivathana (known as Vathana), who grew up in the countryside, learned to respect both nature and the elephants. After choosing to study forestry at his university, he committed himself to the **(4)** ..... of Cambodia's natural resources and began working for the protection of the country's national parks. To begin

with, Vathana focused his attention on understanding the **(5)** ..... the Cambodian farmers were facing. As a result, he came to the **(6)** ..... that the farmers needed to know more about the elephants' migration patterns and how to apply practical solutions for protecting their farms.

First, he helped them build electric fences. Then, he **(7)** ..... them how to use hot chili peppers and other native plants that elephants don't like in order to discourage the animals from eating their crops. Moreover, he **(8)** ..... the farmers to organize themselves to help each other guard their farms at night and to use fireworks and make other loud noises to scare the elephants off. Most **(9)** ..... , he helped farmers improve their farming techniques so they would have no reason to go farther into the elephants' habitat.

	A	B	C	D
1	A simply	B respectfully	C rapidly	D likely
2	A As	B Provided that	C Unless	D Whether or not
3	A lost	B gathered	C damaged	D planted
4	A ecology	B conservation	C habitat	D education
5	A opportunities	B challenges	C tools	D families
6	A realization	B education	C occupation	D notification
7	A asked	B showed	C indicated	D developed
8	A ordered	B changed	C corrected	D advised
9	A importantly	B truthfully	C quickly	D interestingly

LISTENING COMPLETION

▶6:37 **You will hear part of a report. Read the paragraph below. Then listen and complete each statement with the word or short phrase you hear in the report. Listen a second time to check your work.**

Some experts believe the world's total population will increase through 2070. However, it will stabilize and will have (1) .... by that time. They also predict an (2) .... life expectancy and (3) .... birthrates. This will contribute to a (4) .... toward aging populations worldwide, particularly in (5) .... developed countries. According to newsweek.com, one in every six people will be (6) .... over sixty-five by 2050. In fact, there will be (7) .... seniors as children. However, in Africa, the population of children under eighteen years old will (8) .... These challenges will require more funding for children's (9) .... and (10) .... resources for seniors. In addition, more (11) .... will have to be produced for a growing population.

READING COMPLETION
Read the selection. Choose the word or phrase that best completes each statement.

The Other Side of the Story

Although globalization has promised to benefit everyone with an increase in worldwide wealth and prosperity, critics argue that there is **(1)** ..... a widening gap between the rich and the poor. While corporations in some developed countries have outsourced both manufacturing and customer service jobs to developing countries overseas, workers who have lost those jobs **(2)** ..... to make ends meet. On the other hand, India's economy has reaped the **(3)** ..... of globalization with the establishment of call centers, where English-speaking staff provide 24/7 technical support by phone and Internet to customers all over the world. So, more people in India have **(4)** ..... good jobs and a steady income.

Even so, critics of globalization argue that **(5)** ..... free trade has made the world so competitive that criminal activities have flourished. While child labor is illegal in many countries, its practice has increased to fill manufacturing **(6)** ..... for gold and textiles. Recent news reports have exposed the use of slavery on merchant ships, where workers are mistreated and forced to work without receiving any wages. Even worse, due to the fact that there is little international **(7)** ..... regulation, some developing countries are becoming dumping grounds for hazardous industrial waste. In other countries, increased development has brought with it uncontrolled pollution, **(8)** ..... threatens public health and contributes to global warming.

(9) ..... , economic opportunities made possible by globalization have also encouraged government corruption. Some argue that a global economy has helped drug cartels and terrorists move people and materials across borders more easily.

1	**A** either	**B** instead	**C** contrast	**D** neither
2	**A** struggle	**B** demonstrate	**C** apply	**D** interview
3	**A** changes	**B** unemployment	**C** challenges	**D** benefits
4	**A** obtained	**B** lost	**C** searched	**D** desired
5	**A** unwanted	**B** unregulated	**C** inadequate	**D** decreased
6	**A** locations	**B** resources	**C** opportunities	**D** demands
7	**A** environmental	**B** illegal	**C** recognized	**D** agreement
8	**A** which	**B** so that it	**C** since it	**D** and
9	**A** For instance	**B** Even so	**C** As a result	**D** Unfortunately

LISTENING COMPLETION

A ▶6:38 You will hear a report. Read the paragraph below. Then listen and complete each statement with the word or short phrase you hear in the report. Listen a second time to check your work.

The woman says that consumers in (1) .... have been catching up with consumers in (2) .... in purchasing nonessential luxury goods. However, there is concern that the increase in (3) .... of luxury goods will have a (4) .... on the environment. The director of research for Worldwatch warns that supplies of natural resources may (5) ....

B ▶6:39 You will hear a report. Read the paragraph below. Then listen and complete each statement with the word or short phrase you hear in the report. Listen a second time to check your work.

The man reports that a recent survey conducted in more than (6) .... countries shows that people continue to be concerned about (7) .... issues. Specifically, they worry about their country's (8) .... , deteriorating (9) .... , and the growing gap between the (10) .... However, most respondents didn't blame these concerns on (11) ....

THIRD EDITION

SUMMIT 2B

WORKBOOK

JOAN SASLOW
ALLEN ASCHER

UNIT 6 Troubles While Traveling

PREVIEW

1 Complete the chart. Compare and contrast the different types of transportation. What are the advantages and disadvantages of each? Consider the hassles that you face or can avoid with each type.

Type of transportation	Advantages	Disadvantages
car		
plane		
train		
bus		

2 **WHAT ABOUT YOU?** Answer the questions.

1. Which type(s) of transportation do you usually take when you travel? Why?

_____

_____

2. Which type(s) of transportation do you prefer? Why?

_____

_____

THE TEN BEST AIRPORTS IN THE WORLD*

1. Singapore Changi Airport
2. Incheon International Airport (South Korea)
3. Munich Airport (Germany)
4. Hong Kong International Airport
5. Tokyo International Airport (Japan)
6. Zurich Airport (Switzerland)
7. Central Japan International Airport
8. London Heathrow Airport (Great Britain)
9. Amsterdam Schiphol Airport (Netherlands)
10. Beijing Capital International Airport (China)

*Results based on a 31-question survey that asked travelers to rate issues such as wait times and service, ambience and cleanliness, ease of understanding signs, shopping and dining options, and access to public transportation.

3 Complete each conversation with the correct expression.

I'm drawing a blank	it's a safe bet	we'll cross that bridge when we come to it
I'm off	no sweat	
I'm toast	the way I see it	

1. **A:** Are we doing anything this weekend?
   B: It seems like we are, but _____. I just can't remember what it is.

2. **A:** Oh no. I missed the 3:40 train.
   B: Don't worry. I think _____ there's another one leaving soon.

3. **A:** Which cities should we visit on our trip?
   B: Well, _____, we should try to see as much as we can in two weeks.

4. **A:** If I don't get this report done by the end of the day, _____.
   B: Here, I'll help you.

5. **A:** We got to the boarding gate just in time. What if our luggage doesn't make it?
   B: I guess _____.

6. **A:** Oh no! I left my wallet at home.
   B: Oh, _____. I'll lend you money for dinner.

7. **A:** OK, _____.
   B: Safe travels!

4 Choose the correct verb phrases to complete each statement.

1. If we **had taken / would be taking** the train, we **wouldn't sit / wouldn't be sitting** in traffic right now.

2. If she **hadn't talked / hadn't been talking** on her phone, she would **have been hearing / would have heard** the boarding announcement.

3. If the children **had slept / had been sleeping** better, they **wouldn't be arguing / would argue** so much today.

4. If she **isn't traveling / weren't traveling** outside the country, she **wouldn't need / didn't need** her passport.

5. I **wouldn't be using / wouldn't have been using** my cell phone if the plane **would be taking off / were taking off**.

5 Read each statement. Then complete the unreal conditional sentence. Use at least one continuous verb form in each sentence.

1. Alan: It's too bad they overbooked the flight. I was supposed to fly to Spain tonight.

   If they _hadn't overbooked_ (not overbook) the flight, I _would be flying_ (fly) to Spain tonight.

2. Jules: I'm so glad I sat in this seat. I got to meet Sam.

   If Jules _____ (not sit) in this seat, she _____ (not met) Sam.

3. Cara: I wish I'd used the bathroom before we left! Now I can't find one.

   If Cara _____ (use) the bathroom before she left, she _____ (not look) for one now.

4. Rob: I'm glad I'm not hanging out at home tonight. There's nothing to do but watch TV.

   If Rob _____ (hang out) at home tonight, he _____ (watch) TV.

5. Tim and Marcy: We're glad we're traveling during the week. This train is very crowded on the weekend.

   If we _____ (travel) on the weekend, the train _____ (be) much more crowded.

6. Paulo: I wasn't paying attention when I parked the car. Now it's getting towed!

   If Paulo _____ (pay) attention when he parked the car, it _____ (not get) towed right now.

7. Sara and Jeff: We should have packed some snacks to take on the plane. We really don't like this airline food.

   Sara and Jeff _____ (not eat) the airline food now if they _____ (pack) some snacks.

6 WHAT ABOUT YOU? Complete the unreal conditional sentences. Use continuous verb forms and your own ideas.

1. If I were with my family right now, I _____.

2. If it were the weekend, I _____.

3. If I hadn't decided to study English, I _____.

4. If I could be doing anything I wanted right now, I _____.

7 Put the sentences in order. Write the number on the line.

_____ **Brian:** Thanks so much. I really appreciate it.

_____ **Amy:** What's that?

__1__ **Brian:** Amy, could you do me a favor?

_____ **Amy:** Of course not. I'd be happy to.

_____ **Brian:** I've got a horrendous headache. Would you mind getting me some aspirin?

8 Complete each statement of relief or regret, using <u>if it weren't for</u> or <u>if it hadn't been for</u>.

1. _____ the express bus, we would have missed our flight.

2. I would go for a walk with you _____ my sore ankle.

3. _____ Angie, our travel agent, we might have been waiting overnight for a flight.

4. _____ the icy roads, we wouldn't have had an accident.

5. We would be in the museum by now _____ these long lines.

9 Rewrite each statement of relief or regret, using <u>if it weren't for</u> or <u>if it hadn't been for</u>.

1. Without your help, I never would have passed this class.

   _____

2. This would be a perfect flight, except for the uncomfortable seats.

   _____

3. Without the confusion at the airport, our bags wouldn't have gotten lost.

   _____

4. If we didn't have a scheduling conflict, we would go to your party.

   _____

5. We would have gotten lost without that stranger's help.

   _____

10 Write a request for a favor for each picture.

1. _____

_____

2. _____

_____

3. _____

_____

4. _____

_____

5. _____

_____

11 Now choose one of the situations from Exercise 10 and write a conversation in which someone asks for a favor and expresses gratitude. Use the Conversation Spotlight on Student's Book page 67 as a model.

_____

_____

_____

_____

_____

_____

_____

12 Read the interview with an Internet hacker.

The Public Wi-Fi Blues

DD: This is Donald Dean, your roving reporter, going all over the city to give you information on the things that matter in your life. Thanks for listening. I know one of the things that matters to you is security—for your information, for your money, and for your identity. You may feel pretty safe, but in the first six months of this year, there were 1,860 incidents of hacking reported, exposing 228 million records. And we don't know how many went unreported. Of course, most hacking targets business and industry. But you could be a target, too, if you're not careful.

So, today I'm talking to a hacker! Well, she's not really a hacker. Veronica Tyler is a computer security specialist, a real expert. But if she hadn't learned how hackers get into your personal computer, she couldn't help you keep them out. So, Veronica, thank you for agreeing to talk to me and my listeners.

VT: It's my pleasure, Donald.

DD: We're here at Ground Up coffee shop so that you can show me up close what hackers can do in a place like this. Where do we start?

VT: Well, we already took the first step. When we ordered our coffee, we got the Wi-Fi password. Now, I'm turning on my laptop and this clever but nasty little device.

DD: What's it doing? What's that on your monitor?

VT: Information. I'm intercepting signals from laptops, tablets, and smart phones all over the café. This is really basic hacking, and I can already tell you a lot. For example, I can see what Wi-Fi networks each of these people has joined before. And that means I know a lot about them.

DD: Like what?

VT: The guy in the red baseball cap has recently been to Boston. He was logged in to the Logan International Airport network. He stayed at the Morris Hotel, which is very expensive. If I were a real hacker, I would pay close attention to him. He also likes to play golf and eat at fast food places, which are often wi-fi hotspots. But let's get serious now. One of the most effective hacking techniques involves setting up an evil twin.

DD: What in the world is an evil twin?

VT: On a soap opera, it's a character who is supposed to be the twin brother or sister of one of the regular characters. But while the regular character is good and moral, the twin is evil and dangerous.

DD: Okay. If we were talking about soap operas, I would know exactly what you mean. But we're talking about hacking.

VT: And in hacking, an evil twin is a hidden wireless Internet access point that impersonates a legitimate access point. Hackers use it to get sensitive information, like user names and passwords to various accounts.

DD: How does that work?

VT: Well, when someone tries to log in, they see a list of possible networks, right? The name of this coffee shop's Wi-Fi network is on that list, but it's not the same as the name of the shop. It's just a selection of letters and numbers. Now, people are more comfortable with names than with random letter and number combinations. So, on my access point, I've set up another network called GroundUp. It's now on the list, too. Now I'm going to disrupt service for a moment. Okay. Everybody's Wi-Fi connection has gone off. Let's see what happens when people try to reconnect.

DD: They're connecting to GroundUp! The evil twin! So they don't remember or care that what they originally logged in to, the actual coffee shop network, was not named for the shop at all?

VT: No. They happily log in to the evil twin because it's named GroundUp.

DD: I'm afraid I would, too. That's scary.

VT: So, at this point, I can get into their computers and get anything I want. Their online banking credentials, credit card numbers, even Social Security numbers. If it weren't for my honesty and integrity, I could cause a lot of trouble, even do an identity theft. But I couldn't touch the young woman in the green shirt. Her information is encrypted and I wouldn't be able to break the code.

DD: Fascinating. Well, that's all the time we have, Veronica. Thank you for some great information. And now, this is Donald Dean saying, "See you next time."

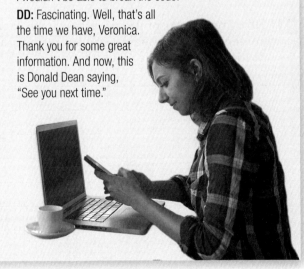

Now answer the questions.

1. What is Veronica Tyler's job? How does she use her hacking skills? _____
   _____

2. What does Tyler's little device allow her to do? _____

3. Why does knowing what Wi-Fi networks people have joined before tell Tyler a lot about them?
   _____

4. Why would a hacker pay close attention to the man in the red baseball cap? _____
   _____

5. What is an evil twin? What does it allow hackers to do? _____
   _____

6. What information *can't* be accessed using the evil twin? _____

7. Before reading this interview, if you were using the Internet, and the Wi-Fi connection were interrupted, do you think you would pay much attention to the name of the network when you logged back in?
   _____

8. Did anything in the interview surprise you? What was it? _____
   _____

13 After reading the interview in Exercise 12, what will you (or should you) do differently the next time you use a public wireless network?

_____

_____

_____

LESSON 4

14 Complete each sentence with the appropriate past participial adjective as a noun modifier.

1. On my last vacation, my luggage was lost. When the airline was unable to locate my
   _____lost_____ luggage, they reimbursed me promptly.

2. A waiter spilled a glass of red wine, staining the front of my dress. I took the the
   _____ dress to the dry cleaners, but they couldn't get the stain out.

3. My son accidentally broke a vase in a souvenir shop. Of course, we had to pay for the
   _____ vase.

4. A thief stole my laptop while I was eating in an outdoor café. Surprisingly, the police caught the thief
   and recovered the _____ laptop within 24 hours.

5. I dropped my new camera and damaged the lens. Luckily, it's still under warranty, so when I called
   customer service they offered to repair or replace the _____ lens.

6. Someone burglarized a suite in the hotel. The police are now searching for evidence in the
   _____ suite.

15 Read the blog post about a lost-luggage experience.

A Travel Nightmare

Posted: June 6

Let me tell you about my recent travel nightmare. I was flying from Tokyo to Boston for my sister's wedding. I was really busy at work the week before I left, so I didn't really have much time to prepare for my trip. If I had been paying more attention to my preparations, I would probably have had a much better trip. Anyway, the night before my flight I packed in a hurry. I had bought a beautiful new dress for the wedding, and I packed that carefully. But after that, I mostly just threw in clothes, the jewelry that I intended to wear to the wedding, and the wedding gift I had bought for my sister and her husband. Other than that, I'm not even sure what I packed.

The next morning I overslept, so I had to race to the airport and ended up checking in late. Because I was so rushed, I forgot to fill out the identification tag that the airline provided for my suitcase. I didn't even wait at the ticketing counter while they put the destination label on my bag; I had to run to the security checkpoint and barely made it onto my plane before they closed the jetway.

Imagine my dismay when I arrived in Boston, after a tight connection in Los Angeles, to discover that my suitcase hadn't arrived with me! I ended up having to buy a new dress for the wedding, but it wasn't as nice as the one I had packed. And I didn't have the gift that I had packed! My suitcase finally arrived three days later, but by then the wedding was over. I suppose it could have been worse—the gift was undamaged, and my sister loved it—but I could have been dancing without a care in the world at the wedding if I had only taken a few precautions.

Kayo

💬 Comment   ➔ Share

Now write the things that Kayo did wrong and the things that she should have done.

_____

_____

_____

_____

_____

If you've ever lost your luggage on a trip, then you know it can be a nightmare to recover it. Despite airlines' efforts to reduce the number of lost bags, hundreds of thousands of pieces of luggage still go missing every year, a great deal of which is never reclaimed. What happens to all that stuff? Much of it is bought for a minimal price and resold by a store called the Unclaimed Baggage Center. Each year the store sells millions of items, including suitcases, clothing, cameras, and jewelry, for a fraction of their retail value.

GRAMMAR BOOSTER

A Read each conditional sentence. Then read each pair of statements that follow. Check True or False.

		True	False
1.	If Dave were here, he'd tell us what to do.		
	Dave is here.	☐	☐
	Dave is going to tell us what to do.	☐	☐
2.	If she hadn't read the letter, she would have been shocked by the news.		
	She didn't read the letter.	☐	☐
	She wasn't shocked by the news.	☐	☐
3.	We might be on the train now if we hadn't gotten stuck in traffic.		
	We're not on the train.	☐	☐
	We got stuck in traffic.	☐	☐
4.	If I have time, I may be able to help you out.		
	I am certain that I'll have time.	☐	☐
	I will definitely help you out.	☐	☐
5.	If he had taken my advice, he wouldn't be in trouble.		
	He took my advice.	☐	☐
	He's in trouble.	☐	☐

B Choose the correct word or phrase to complete each sentence.

1. If the park gets too full, you _____ wait for some people to leave before they let anyone else in.
    a. had to
    b. wouldn't have had to
    c. have to
    d. didn't have to

2. The air-conditioning automatically turns on if the temperature _____ above 27 degrees Celsius.
    a. goes
    b. will go
    c. would go
    d. would have gone

3. If we had gotten the call earlier, we _____ help.
    a. would
    b. will
    c. were going to
    d. might have been able to

4. Kyle studied very hard for his test. But if he _____, he would be really nervous.
    a. had studied
    b. would have studied
    c. hadn't studied
    d. doesn't study

5. I _____ so excited to go to Paris tomorrow if I had been there before.
    a. wouldn't have been
    b. wouldn't be
    c. won't be
    d. hadn't been

6. If we had time, we _____ the Grand Canyon.
    a. would visit
    b. would have visited
    c. visited
    d. visit

7. I _____ you if you help me first.
    a. helped
    b. will help
    c. had helped
    d. would have helped

8. If Jon _____ on our team, we would have won the game.
   a. would have been
   b. wouldn't have been
   c. had been
   d. was

9. Heather _____ surprised right now if you hadn't told her about the party.
   a. is
   b. had been
   c. will be
   d. would be

10. If the weather _____ bad, we'll move the party inside.
    a. was
    b. had been
    c. were
    d. is

C **WHAT ABOUT YOU? Complete the conditional sentences in your own way.**

1. If I had more free time, _____

   _____

2. If we arrive at English class late, _____

   _____

3. If I hadn't decided to _____

   _____

4. If I spoke English fluently, _____

   _____

WRITING A comparison and contrast essay

A **PREWRITING: COMPARE & CONTRAST CHART** Complete the chart below to compare two vacation destinations that you'd like to visit. Write each destination name at the top of the chart. Then fill in the chart with how the destinations are similar and how they are different.

COMPARING VACATION DESTINATIONS

DESTINATION 1: ______________________	DESTINATION 2: ______________________

Similarities

____

____

____

Differences

______________________	______________________
______________________	______________________
______________________	______________________

B **WRITING** On a separate sheet of paper, compare and contrast the two places. Use the information in your diagram. Explain which place you think you'd prefer to visit for a vacation. Use expressions of comparison and contrast.

C **SELF-CHECK**

- ☐ Did I use expressions of comparison and contrast?
- ☐ Does my essay have an introductory and a concluding paragraph?
- ☐ Do the supporting paragraphs follow one of the formats illustrated in the Student's Book on page 72?

WRITING MODEL

Two places that I'd love to visit for a vacation are Nice in France and Cinque Terre in Italy. Both are very beautiful places and great vacation destinations. However, there are some differences.

Nice is a busy beach city. There are people from all over the world shopping, eating in world-class restaurants, and going to dance clubs that stay open very late. Similarly, Cinque Terre is also on the water, but the environment is very different. It is still undiscovered by many tourists. In contrast to the fast pace of Nice, most of the visitors to Cinque Terre spend their days hiking, swimming, and visiting olive groves and vineyards.

Both Nice and Cinque Terre are great for vacation. But if I had to choose just one of those places, I think I would choose Cinque Terre. For me, it'd probably be more relaxing.

1 Look at the photos. Which photos show a real situation or event as it actually occurred when the photo was taken? Which photos have been changed using a computer? Are there any that you're not sure about? Write your reactions below.

1. _____

2. _____

3. _____

4. _____

5. _____

6. _____

2 Look back at what you wrote in Exercise 1. Do you think "seeing is believing"? When you see photos online or in newspapers, how do you decide which are "real"?

_____

_____

_____

_____

3 Complete the conversations with expressions from the box.

don't get me wrong	if I were in your shoes	the cat's out of the bag
I may be imagining things	keep in mind	what's on your mind

1. **A:** Can I talk to you for a sec?

   B: Of course. _____?

2. **A:** _____, but I think something's bothering Tina.

   B: Really? _____ that she's really busy at work right now. It might just be that.

3. **A:** I'm trying to decide whether to ask my boss for a raise or not.

   B: _____, I would definitely ask. You deserve one.

4. **A:** Wow, look at this amazing photo!

   B: Hmm. It looks a little fake to me. _____. It's beautiful, but I just think it's been manipulated to make it more colorful.

5. **A:** Gina, is that a new ring you're wearing?

   B: Actually, it is. I was going to make an announcement at dinner, but I guess _____. Jim and I are getting married!

LESSON 1

4 Write <u>a</u>, <u>an</u>, or <u>the</u> before the noun where necessary. Write _X_ if the noun should not have an article. Then write <u>definite</u>, <u>indefinite</u>, <u>unique</u>, or <u>generic</u>.

1. __The__ ingredients in this soup are all organic. __definite__

2. _____ CEO of our company announced budget cuts. _____

3. _____ Apples are a very popular fruit. _____

4. You should eat _____ apple a day. _____

5. _____ rain is coming down really hard now. _____

6. It's so dry out. Our garden needs _____ rain. _____

7. _____ scam that fooled you also fooled me. _____

5 Complete the sentences. Insert <u>a</u>, <u>an</u>, or <u>the</u> before a noun or noun phrase where necessary. Write *X* if the noun should not have an article.

1. Phishing is _____ scam designed to steal a person's identity. Victims of _____ scam receive _____ e-mail that appears to come from _____ trusted website such as their bank or favorite shopping site. _____ e-mail attempts to trick people into disclosing valuable personal information like credit card numbers, passwords, or account data.

2. Until the 1800s, British doctors believed that _____ tomatoes were poisonous and caused conditions like "brain fever" and cancer. In fact, _____ tomato is highly nutritious and a good source of vitamin A, which is important for healthy hair and skin.

3. There's _____ new product being marketed on _____ Internet called "Exercise in a Bottle." In pop-up ads, the company claims that _____ product will burn fat while the user is just sitting around doing nothing or even sleeping. _____ ads also state that consumers can enjoy fried chicken, pizza, and other high-calorie, high-fat products and still lose weight.

4. _____ U.S.-based company is in the business of selling stars. For $48 you can purchase _____ star and name it. _____ company has faced a great deal of criticism from _____ astrologers and consumer groups, who point out that the certificates of purchase issued by the company aren't recognized by any other organization. "They can't sell _____ sun because it's not theirs to sell," states one critic of the company.

6 WHAT ABOUT YOU? Describe an ad you've seen that you suspect is a scam. Explain why you don't buy it.

_____

_____

_____

_____

7 Have you ever received an e-mail or phone call that was a scam? Describe the message that you received. What did you do?

_____

_____

_____

_____

8 Read the article. Then choose the best answer to complete each statement.

Aisle or Window Seat? Superstitious or Non-superstitious?

In today's scientific world, many people are reluctant to admit to believing in superstitions. But talk to a few people in the travel industry, and you'll soon learn that superstition is alive and well around the world.

In much of the Western world, it's long been thought that the number 13 is bad luck. Next time you're traveling by air, try looking for row number 13 on your airplane. Chances are, there isn't one. Few airlines have a row 13, and most airlines don't offer flight numbers that contain that number. The airlines offer different reasons for this. One airline spokesperson noted that the taboo associated with the number 13 is an old tradition that has persisted only because it would be too expensive to renumber the rows on hundreds of airplanes.

A spokesperson for a different airline admitted that the airline omits row 13 because too many passengers refuse to sit in those seats. Travel industry studies even show that travel declines on "unlucky" days, such as the thirteenth day of the month.

In parts of Asia, the number 4 is considered unlucky because it has a similar pronunciation to that of the Chinese word for "death." In Japan, the number 9 is avoided because it sounds like the Japanese word for "torture." Some Asian airlines skip these numbers when numbering airplane rows. (Curiously, although the number 13 is not considered unlucky by most Asians, row 13 is also often skipped.) Visit Seoul's Incheon Airport, and you'll notice that there are no gates numbered 4, 13, or 44.

Superstitions about numbers can also be positive. In China, it's said that the number 8 is lucky because

✈ DEPARTURES		
Time	Destination	Flight
19:30	BEIJING	R4 4509
19:30	ATLANTA	EB 7134
19:45	LONDON	DN 0045
19:40	NEW YORK	OD 7158
19:50	FRANKFURT	NP 6890
20:05	DUBAI	UC 1207
20:10	CHICAGO	EB 3436
20:20	TOKYO	R4 4581
20:45	PARIS	NP 1976

its pronunciation is similar to that of the Chinese word that means "to strike it rich." When one airline recently introduced a flight from Beijing to Newark, they named it Flight 88 and offered a "lucky" $888 round-trip ticket price. In the United States, where it is believed that the numbers 7 and 11 bring good fortune, flight numbers containing these numbers are very common for flights to the gambling casinos of Las Vegas.

Superstitious behavior isn't limited to passengers—flight attendants and flight crew have a reputation for being superstitious, too. Some have been known to refuse hotel rooms whose numbers coincided with those of flights that ended in tragedy.

Whether our superstitions are rooted in tradition or personal experience, it seems that most of us pack them up and take them with us, no matter where in the world we travel.

1. The article _____.
   a. offers advice on avoiding bad luck on a trip
   b. recommends that the travel industry change policies that are based on superstitions
   c. explains how superstitions affect the travel industry

2. _____ is considered by many travelers to be unlucky.
   a. A seat in the thirteenth row of an airplane
   b. An airline flight number that contains the number 8
   c. An airport gate numbered 7

3. The article claims that _____.
    a. passengers are more superstitious than flight attendants
    b. Asian travelers are more superstitious than travelers from other parts of the world
    c. some passengers avoid traveling on days of the month that are considered unlucky

4. The article does not claim that _____.
    a. believing in superstitions is old-fashioned
    b. superstitions exist all over the world
    c. some airlines choose lucky flight numbers to increase ticket sales

9 **WHAT ABOUT YOU?** **Answer the questions.**

1. What numbers are considered lucky or unlucky in your country? Can you explain why?

    _____

    _____

2. Are there any numbers that you personally consider lucky or unlucky? Why or why not?

    _____

    _____

10 **Replace the subject and active verb in each statement with <u>it</u> + a passive reporting verb.**

1. Many people believe that hanging a horseshoe with ends pointing up brings good luck.

    _____ that hanging a horseshoe with ends pointing up brings good luck.

2. They say that picking up a penny on the sidewalk will bring good luck.

    _____ that picking up a penny on the sidewalk will bring good luck.

3. Estimates are that 25% of Americans are superstitious.

    _____ that 25% of Americans are superstitious.

4. People once thought that lightning during a summer storm caused crops to ripen.

    _____ that lightning during a summer storm caused crops to ripen.

5. In some countries, people believe that standing chopsticks upright in a bowl of rice is a symbol of death.

    In some countries, _____ that standing chopsticks upright in a bowl of rice is a symbol of death.

6. People used to say that taking someone's picture was like taking his or her soul.

    _____ that taking someone's picture was like taking his or her soul.

7. People used to believe that a clap of thunder after a funeral meant that the person's soul had reached its final resting place.

8. _____ that a clap of thunder after a funeral meant that the person's soul had reached its final resting place.

11 **What are some superstitions that you know of? Complete the sentences.**

1. In some cultures, it is considered good luck _____.

2. In some cultures, _____ is considered to be bad luck.

3. The numbers _____ are thought to be _____ luck in some countries.

4. An animal that is believed to be good luck in _____ is the _____.

5. If you want your baby to be _____, you should _____.

12 Read the article about visualization as used by elite athletes.

Visualizing the Way to Victory

It's often said that sports are 90 percent mental and 10 percent physical. It may be a cliché, but many athletes and trainers now place a strong emphasis on the mental aspect of training. As many elite athletes will tell you, mental toughness and focus is often the difference that separates the very best (think Olympic gold medal) athletes from the second-best. For almost all elite athletes, visualization, or as some prefer to call it, using imagery, is now a crucial part of their training.

What is visualization? In a nutshell, it involves mentally simulating every aspect of an event, competition, or race. It can be thought of as "athletic training for the brain." Athletes use visualization to build focus, reduce stress, and tune out distractions. While visualization cannot replace physical practice, it can greatly enhance it. Studies have shown that the brain patterns activated when someone visualizes performing a sport are the same brain patterns as those activated by actually doing the sport.

"Visualization might be a misleading term, since using mental imagery involves all five senses," says sports psychologist Dr. Dana Carter. Athletes focus on how things feel, smell, and sound as they go through every moment of their event in their mind. For example, a bobsledder will visualize his or her way down the bobsled track, slowing down the process and "seeing" every inch of the track. "Athletes are actually feeling the ice or the track beneath them, feeling the wind hit their skin, seeing the turns in the track or the moguls on the mountain, hearing their skates on the ice or their body in the water," says Carter. Many athletes even move their bodies as they practice mental imagery because their muscles are responding to the brain signals created as they visualize themselves performing. "It can be a little weird to watch," says Chelsea Yost, an elite skier who has worked with Dr. Carter. "People might be moving their arms, bouncing back and forth, all with their eyes closed and this look of intense concentration on their faces."

Another aspect of mental imagery is known as instructional self-talk. As athletes imagine themselves going through the motions of their event, they tell themselves what to do, step by step—for example, "Point your toes," "Glide, then pull," or "Push off quickly, arms up." Some athletes record this step-by-step instruction aloud, along with what they're seeing and feeling at every moment. They then play it back over and over, feeling muscles in their bodies responding as they would during the actual event. It's believed that mental exercises like this actually train the muscles to respond more quickly.

Yet another aspect of mental imaging is called "pattern-breaking." Pattern- breaking uses imagery to get rid of fear or nervousness. For example, if an athlete has had an accident or been injured while competing, images of the trauma may pop into his or her head before a similar competition. With practice, visualization can help the athlete push out the negative images. Some athletes use an image of a physical action, such as a balloon popping or an elastic band snapping, that they can summon up as a "trigger" to dispel the negative thoughts. Once athletes become adept at pattern-breaking, they are able to banish negative thoughts and maintain positive focus much more easily, which is crucial in competition.

Visualization is not just for elite athletes. Studies have shown that it significantly improves performance in beginning athletes as well. But you need to do more than just think about performing your sport. You need to focus on every little detail: how every moment of the event feels, sounds, looks, smells. Slow down and imagine each step in the event, or in a portion of the event, such as the beginning of a race, or the last hundred yards. You never know—it may give you just the edge over the local competition that you need in your next 5K race!

Now answer the questions.

1. In your own words, what is visualization, or mental imagery? _____

_____

2. How is it used by athletes? _____

_____

3. What is instructional self-talk? _____

_____

4. What effect might instructional self-talk have on the body? _____

_____

5. What is pattern-breaking? _____

_____

6. When using pattern-breaking, what images might be used as a "trigger"? _____

_____

7. How can pattern-breaking be valuable in competition? _____

_____

8. How is visualization different from just thinking about performing a sport? _____

_____

13 **WHAT ABOUT YOU?** Answer the questions.

1. Name a sport or an activity that you do. If you were to try visualization, what details would you need to imagine?

_____

_____

2. If you were to try instructional self-talk, what words or phrases might you use?

_____

_____

3. In what situations could pattern-breaking help you overcome fear or nervousness?

_____

_____

4. What image might you visualize as your trigger to help you banish your fearful thoughts?

_____

_____

LESSON 4

14 Complete the conversation between two friends. Use the expressions from the box. Change verb forms and pronouns as necessary.

be all in one's mind	make up one's mind
be out of one's mind	~~put (something) out of one's mind~~
change one's mind	

Kelly: Hey, let's go to a spa on Saturday. We can relax and enjoy ourselves. Let's forget about work and _put it out of our minds_ .

1.

Andrea: That sounds great, but I can't. I'm going to a class. Actually, it's a seminar—to help me get over my fear of dogs.

Kelly: Really? I didn't know you were afraid of dogs.

Andrea: Yeah. I know my fear isn't really logical or real, and it _____, but I've had trouble getting over it.

2.

Kelly: So what made you decide to try to get over your fear now?

Andrea: Well, it's a little embarrassing. People think I _____ when I'm terrified of a tiny dog.

3.

Kelly: Everyone's afraid of something.

Andrea: I know, but it's still hard. Everyone in my family loves dogs, and they each have at least one. So I've _____ that I want

4.

to get over my fear so I can go visit them.

Kelly: Well, good luck with the class. And if you _____

5.

about going to the spa, let me know.

15 Read the conversation in Exercise 14 again. Then check <u>True</u> or <u>False</u> for each statement.

	True	False
1. Kelly suggests visiting a spa to relieve work-related stress.	☐	☐
2. Kelly has a phobia.	☐	☐
3. Andrea thinks that her fear of dogs is irrational.	☐	☐
4. Kelly thinks Andrea's fear is crazy and foolish.	☐	☐
5. Andrea has decided to try to overcome her fear.	☐	☐
6. Andrea's fear of dogs is interfering with her life.	☐	☐

16 **WHAT ABOUT YOU?** Answer the questions.

1. List a few things that many people are afraid of. Why do you think people fear these things?

Common fear	Reason
bees	bee stings are painful

2. Do you know anyone who has an irrational phobia? Do you feel sympathy for that person? Why or why not?

_____

_____

3. What advice would you give to someone who wants to get over a phobia?

_____

_____

17 Complete each sentence with the correct word from Student's Book page 83.

1. Kate is an _____. She wouldn't even go near the window of our high-rise apartment.

2. I have _____. I even get scared in elevators unless they're very large.

3. Trey is _____. That's why he won't travel to other countries.

4. Ariana is an _____. She refuses to fly; she always travels by car.

5. Bill must be _____. A little spider landed on him, and he screamed.

6. If you're an _____, don't go in the reptile house at the zoo!

7. Ken prefers small, enclosed spaces. I think he's a little _____.

Glossophobia,

or the fear of public speaking, is believed to be the most common phobia in the world, affecting as many as 75 percent of all people.

GRAMMAR BOOSTER

A Complete the sentences with **a** or **the**. Write **X** if the noun should not have an article.

1. People in different parts of _____ world have varied superstitions. For example, in some cultures _____ number 13 is considered unlucky, while in others 4 is an unlucky number, and in still others 17 is thought to be _____ bad luck.

2. Bill gave me _____ glass of water to drink. He said that _____ water at his house goes through _____ special filtering system.

3. Lucy bought _____ car last month. _____ car isn't brand new; she bought it from _____ neighbor who had driven it for less than _____ year. But it's in _____ good condition, and Lucy thinks she paid _____ fair price for it.

4. If you're in the mood for Japanese food, I know _____ good restaurant that's not too far from here. _____ restaurant just opened recently, but it's already become one of _____ most popular places in town.

5. _____ success that Jackie has had is because she's _____ hard worker. It has nothing to do with _____ luck.

6. According to _____ recent news program, _____ rich in this country are getting richer, while _____ poor are getting poorer.

B Complete each sentence with a word from the box. Add **a** if necessary. Each word may be used more than once.

fear	superstition	time	victory

1. I remember _____ when life was simpler. Things were very different then.
2. Deborah Richard's election to the presidency represents _____ for women.
3. There's evidence of interest and belief in _____ in cultures worldwide.
4. Hearing the strange noise, we all felt alarmed and looked at one other with _____.
5. Athletes experience the joys of _____ as well as the pains of defeat.
6. According to _____ that I just recently heard, it's bad luck to walk under a ladder.
7. Neil is afraid of flying. It's _____ he's had since he was a child.
8. Do you have _____ to go get something to eat?

C **Rewrite each sentence in the passive voice.**

1. The newspaper reported that the politicians were getting close to a deal.

   The politicians _____.

2. They say that tennis player has never lost a match when wearing his lucky tennis shoes.

   That tennis player _____.

3. Most people think my doctor is one of the best in the country.

   My doctor _____.

4. They say that scams affect elderly people far more than the rest of the population.

   Scams _____.

5. In the past, people didn't think the brain had much effect on physical performance.

   In the past, the brain _____.

A **PREWRITING: "FREEWRITING" FOR IDEAS**

- Choose a fear that you have. On a separate sheet of paper, write for five to ten minutes any words, phrases, statements, or questions about the topic that come to mind.

- Consider exactly what you are afraid of, where the fear came from, how it makes you feel, how it affects your life, and how you might overcome it.

- Write quickly. Do not take time to correct spelling, punctuation, organization, etc.

- Read what you wrote. Circle ideas that go together and add more details.

B **WRITING** On a separate sheet of paper, describe your fear. Use your freewriting notes for ideas.

WRITING MODEL

I'm afraid of upsetting other people. It's not a fear that actually causes me fright—for me it's more like I feel very nervous about doing something that someone else won't like. This fear probably stems from my childhood when my mother insisted that I always consider how my words and actions would affect other people. Now I rarely do anything without thinking about what other people will think.

This fear is actually a bit annoying because it means that I feel inhibited to do a lot of things that other people do easily. For example, if I receive poor service at a restaurant, I likely won't complain because I think the waiter will get angry with me. I know in my head this doesn't make much sense, but it still feels real for me.

I want to overcome my fear, and I think the way to do that is by doing things that I'm afraid of or anxious about. I think that little by little I might be able to overcome my fear.

C **SELF-CHECK**

☐ Did I introduce the topic of my fear in general in my first paragraph?

☐ Did all my paragraphs include topic sentences?

☐ Did all my subjects and verbs agree?

UNIT

8

PREVIEW

Performing at Your Best

1 **Read the tips for improving emotional intelligence.**

Emotional Intelligence

Sign In | Home | |

Issues
ADHD
Addiction
Anger Management
Anxiety
Child or Adolescent
Depression
Eating Disorders
Relationship Issues
More +

Treatment Orientation
Cognitive Behavioral
(CBT)
Dialectical (DBT)
EMDR
Online Therapy
More +

Video Counseling
See Nearest

Support Groups
Psychiatrists
Treatment Centers

Would you like to improve your emotional intelligence? Or do you already have a high EQ? No matter where we fall on the emotional intelligence spectrum, most of us could probably benefit from keeping these tips in mind.

1. Follow the old maxim "Think before you speak." Before you tell someone that you're angry about something they've said or done, take a deep breath and count to ten. Chances are you'll calm down enough to find a more positive way to explain your feelings than if you had spoken immediately.

2. Don't take things personally. If your friend said he would text you and he hasn't, it might not have anything to do with you; he might just be busy. Learning to look at situations in a way that isn't centered around yourself can make you calmer and less likely to see things negatively.

3. Practice empathy. This means "putting yourself in someone else's shoes," or imagining the situation from that person's perspective. Often this helps you to understand why other people behave the way they do. Once you understand where people are coming from, it's easier to get along with them.

4. Examine your weaknesses. Be honest with yourself. It's okay to have weaknesses; we all do. Once you know what yours are, you can work on improving them. If you ignore your weaknesses, or worse yet, pretend you don't have any, you'll never have the opportunity to improve.

5. Think about how you react under stress. Do you get more upset than the situation calls for? If so, try some relaxation techniques, such as deep breathing, yoga, or meditation to help you calm down.

Remember: It is possible to improve your EQ. All it takes is a little honesty with yourself and a little work.

Based on the article, write advice for each person.

1. "My assistant came to the meeting without the copies I had asked her to make. They were an important part of my presentation, and I was angry that I wasn't able to hand them out at the meeting. Unfortunately, I yelled at him in front of everyone. I felt bad immediately."

_____

_____

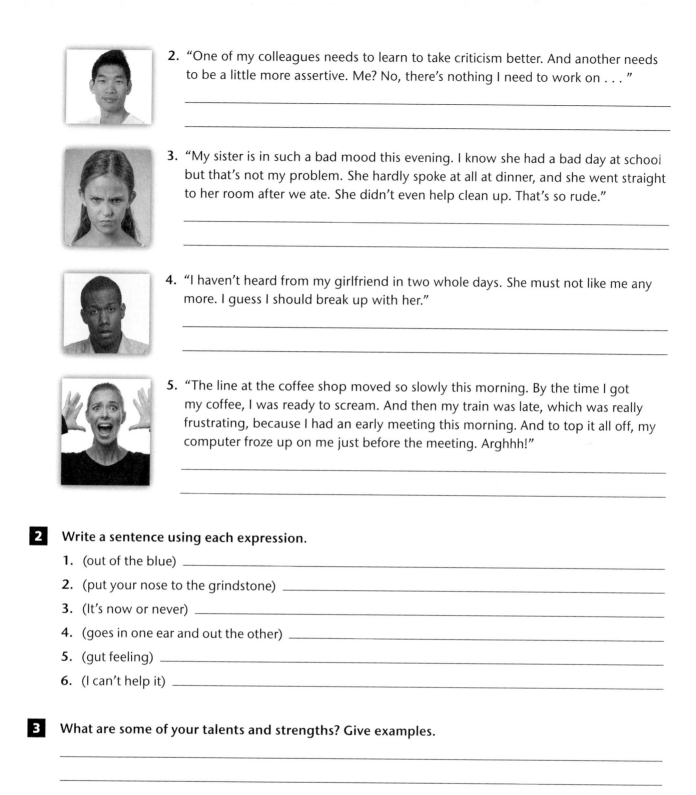

2. "One of my colleagues needs to learn to take criticism better. And another needs to be a little more assertive. Me? No, there's nothing I need to work on . . . "

_____

_____

3. "My sister is in such a bad mood this evening. I know she had a bad day at school but that's not my problem. She hardly spoke at all at dinner, and she went straight to her room after we ate. She didn't even help clean up. That's so rude."

_____

_____

4. "I haven't heard from my girlfriend in two whole days. She must not like me any more. I guess I should break up with her."

_____

_____

5. "The line at the coffee shop moved so slowly this morning. By the time I got my coffee, I was ready to scream. And then my train was late, which was really frustrating, because I had an early meeting this morning. And to top it all off, my computer froze up on me just before the meeting. Arghhh!"

_____

_____

2 Write a sentence using each expression.

1. (out of the blue) _____

2. (put your nose to the grindstone) _____

3. (It's now or never) _____

4. (goes in one ear and out the other) _____

5. (gut feeling) _____

6. (I can't help it) _____

3 What are some of your talents and strengths? Give examples.

_____

_____

_____

_____

4 Read the descriptions of the zodiac signs. Then find your sign. Do you think your strengths and weaknesses match those described? Explain your answer.

_____

_____

Characteristics of the Zodiac Signs

 AQUARIUS (January 20–February 18) You are intelligent and inventive. With an independent (and rebellious) mind, you have your own unique way of thinking and refuse to follow the crowd. You have a talent for discovering new ways of doing things. You love electronic gadgets and figuring out how they work. Your unusual lifestyle and unpredictable nature may seem odd to some people.

 PISCES (February 19–March 20) You have a vivid imagination and have a talent for writing poetry, creating art, and performing on stage. You care deeply for other people and devote time to helping those who are sick. A daydreamer, you have a habit of seeing life as you want it to be, rather than how it really is. You sometimes allow your emotions to control your behavior.

 ARIES (March 21–April 19) You are adventurous and not afraid to try new things. You are always busy and never lazy. You prefer to work independently and don't have patience with people who are slower or less talented. You're not afraid to fight with others to achieve your goals. In your enthusiasm to get things done, you sometimes work too quickly and don't notice smaller points.

 TAURUS (April 20–May 20) You have a fondness for luxury and relaxation. You have excellent taste in food, art, and music. After hearing a song just once, you can sing the lyrics or play the melody. Slow to act and speak, you view all sides of a situation before making decisions, and you choose your words carefully. Although some may find you too quiet, you are a loyal friend.

 GEMINI (May 21–June 20) A smooth talker, you have the ability to communicate ideas clearly and persuade others to agree with your point of view. Always the life of the party, you have many friends. You are skilled at using tools and fixing machines. Your love of talk sometimes gives you the reputation of being a gossip.

 CANCER (June 21–July 22) You are sensitive and emotional. Your love of family is strong, as is your need to protect and care for the people close to you. When making decisions, you have a talent for sensing the correct choice. However, you have a tendency to allow your emotions to get in the way of rational judgments. Shy and easily hurt, you are slow to make friends.

LEO (July 23–August 22) You are a born leader and others naturally look to you for advice and inspiration. An independent spirit, you don't like being told what to do. You love being the center of attention and dislike being ignored. You enjoy playing sports of all kinds, especially in front of an audience. Your desire to be a star sometimes causes you to forget to be a team player.

VIRGO (August 23–September 22) A perfectionist, you are highly critical of anything that is not done properly. You notice small things that less perceptive people miss. You pick up foreign languages easily. You are highly organized and dislike messiness. With your irresistible urge to improve everything and everyone, you are sometimes seen by others as being fussy and narrow-minded.

LIBRA (September 23–October 22) Easygoing and charming, you get along with almost everyone. A skilled diplomat, you are good at solving problems and convincing people to compromise. You have a need for peace and avoid conflict and arguments. Because you always see both sides of any issue, you have difficulty making decisions.

SCORPIO (October 23–November 21) Watchful and perceptive, you quickly sense other people's true thoughts or feelings. You are a good judge of people and a patient listener. However, you are intensely private, and hold back expressing your own emotions. This lack of openness prevents others from getting to know you well.

SAGITTARIUS (November 22–December 21) Fun-loving and free-spirited, you are happiest when on the move or trying new things. You learn foreign languages easily, and your open-mindedness about other cultures makes travel a rewarding experience. A natural storyteller, you love recounting your adventures, although you often exaggerate the facts. You are easily bored.

CAPRICORN (December 22–January 19) Disciplined and hardworking, you know how to get things done. Determined to succeed, you set goals for yourself and patiently take steps until you achieve them. Shy and cautious with new people, you are often uncomfortable in social situations. You prefer to work independently and have trouble asking others for help.

The head of the Vatican library, Cardinal Giuseppe Mezzofanti (1774-1849), had a real knack for languages. It's believed that when he died at the age of 75, he spoke at least 40 languages fluently. This accomplishment is particularly remarkable considering that the Cardinal never traveled outside of Italy. All his learning came from practice with visitors to the Vatican and from books.

5 Read the statements. Check <u>True</u> or <u>False</u>, according to the information presented in the zodiac descriptions in Exercise 4.

	True	False
1. Aries signs have an eye for detail.	☐	☐
2. Taurus signs have an ear for music.	☐	☐
3. Gemini and Aquarius signs tend to be mechanically inclined.	☐	☐
4. Pisces signs have a way with words.	☐	☐
5. Leo, Libra, and Gemini signs have a way with people.	☐	☐
6. Virgo signs have a head for figures.	☐	☐
7. Sagittarius signs have a knack for learning languages.	☐	☐
8. Capricorn signs have a way with people.	☐	☐
9. Aquarius and Scorpio signs have a good intuitive sense.	☐	☐
10. Gemini signs are not good with their hands.	☐	☐

6 Read the conversations. Write a sentence about the strengths and/or weaknesses of each person. Use the Vocabulary from Student's Book page 88. There may be more than one correct answer.

Conversation 1

Ray: Thanks again for helping me out with those calculations today.

Diana: No problem. Glad to help.

Ray: You know, I wish I were good at numbers like you.

Diana: Do you? Actually, I'm envious of your talent for learning languages.

Ray: Really? But languages are easy to learn!

Diana: Not for me. I took four years of French and can't even make a sentence!

(Ray) <u>Ray has a knack for learning languages.</u>

(Diana) _____

Conversation 2

Aidan: Hey, Dave. Nice job on the presentation you gave this afternoon. You got your ideas across really well.

Dave: Thanks. I appreciate that.

Aidan: I could never stand up in front of a big group and give a speech.

Dave: It's not that hard, once you get used to it. It just takes practice.

Aidan: You're probably right, but I think I'll just stick to fixing computers.

Dave: Well, you're really good at that.

(Aidan) _____

(Dave) _____

Conversation 3

Darla: Your scarf is beautiful.

Emily: Thanks. I made it myself.

Darla: You're kidding!

Emily: No. I love doing arts-and-crafts projects.

Darla: Wow, you're so talented. I love the intricate weave.

Emily: Thanks. I can't believe you noticed that. Most people wouldn't pay attention to such a minor part of the design.

(Darla) _____

(Emily) _____

Conversation 4

Andy: Ugh! This stupid watch stopped running again!

Ethan: I can take a look at it if you want. I'm pretty good at fixing things like that. Anyway, I'm sick and tired of studying. I'm never going to remember all these dates for my exam.

Andy: Why don't you make up a song to help you remember them? Put the words to a tune. That's how I usually remember things.

Ethan: That sounds like your area of expertise, not mine. I tell you what: I'll take a look at your watch, and you can help me come up with a song.

(Andy) _____

(Ethan) _____

Conversation 5

Joseph: Congratulations, Barbara. I heard you set another sales record. How do you do it?

Barbara: Honestly, I just seem to know what people want to hear, even without knowing much about them. That makes the sales pitch easy.

Joseph: You make it sound simple, but I could never be a salesperson. Convincing people to buy something just isn't one of my talents.

Barbara: Well, not everyone's a people person.

(Joseph) _____

(Barbara) _____

7 Complete the sentences in your own way. Use <u>do</u> or <u>did</u> for emphasis.

1. I don't have an ear for music. I _do like to listen to it, though._____

2. Sam doesn't have a way with words. He _____.

3. Even though we didn't make it to your art show, we _____.

4. I don't usually have a way with people. I _____.

5. Luke doesn't have a knack for learning languages. He _____.

6. _____. I didn't like her mother, though.

LESSON 2

8 Mark grammatically correct sentences with a checkmark. Mark incorrect sentences with an *X*. Then correct the incorrect sentences.

1. __*X*__ A psychologist suggested that Kim ~~reduces~~ *reduce* her stress levels.

2. _____ It is agreed that measuring intelligence is very complicated.

3. _____ The company will insist that people will not smoke on company property.

4. _____ I've suggested that she talk to her doctor about ways to stimulate her brain's activity.

5. _____ It's important that you be willing to try new things.

6. _____ If you demand that your daughter doesn't keep secrets from you, she'll want to share things

   with you even less.

7. _____ It's desirable that no one knows the details of the project before it is announced.

8. _____ It's essential that each person remembers his or her role in the process.

9. _____ I feel it's necessary that you be aware of how your actions affect others.

10. _____ They recommended that everyone be sleeping well the night before the test.

"It is not enough to have a good mind; the main thing is to use it well."
—René Descartes, 1596–1650, French mathematician, philosopher, and scientist

9 Why do you think tests that measure IQ (intelligence quotient) might not be the best way to predict a person's success in work or life?

_____

_____

_____

_____

_____

_____

_____

JOURNAL OF WORLD SCIENCE

"Intelligence" Isn't Universal

In a recent study, Ph.D.s Robert Sternberg and Elena Grigorenko of Yale University evaluated the accuracy of traditional IQ tests in measuring the intelligence of people in non-Western countries. Although these IQ tests have been successful in accurately predicting academic and career success in many Western countries, the study indicated that they may not accurately assess intelligence in other areas of the world. The study suggests that tests devised for Western cultures fail to take into account the different ways that other cultures define and reward intelligence. According to the researchers, if we truly want to measure intelligence, it's essential that we test for different types of intelligence.

The researchers used Sternberg's Triarchic Theory of Human Intelligence to assess aptitudes of children in different cultures. This model identifies three distinct types of intelligence: crystallized, practical, and creative. According to Sternberg's definitions, *crystallized intelligence* refers to academic knowledge and skills. *Practical intelligence* involves the ability to understand and deal with everyday tasks. *Creative intelligence* is a person's ability to react to new situations. According to Sternberg, it's important that we value all three of these types.

Results showed that Kenyan children who demonstrated high practical intelligence performed poorly in areas of crystallized intelligence. The researchers suggest that the reasons for this may lie in Kenyan culture. Some children are kept at home instead of being sent to school. These children, consequently, are more exposed to their indigenous culture. They learn practical skills such as identifying and using medicinal herbs. Since they do not attend school, however, they may feel uncomfortable when placed in a school environment. They score poorly on academic tests of their native language and English. Therefore, standard IQ tests which only assess crystallized intelligence may not accurately test a Kenyan child's full cognitive abilities.

Similarly, the researchers found that in Russia, a country that has recently experienced many social changes, women with high levels of practical intelligence were better able to cope with changing social conditions than other women. If a woman had strong practical abilities, she usually felt more in control of her own life despite the changes going on around her. Even if a woman scored high in crystallized intelligence, this score alone didn't predict life success in this particular culture.

Based on the results of their studies, the researchers advised that we not assume that the cognitive skills valued and useful in one culture are the same as those valued by another. Therefore, they recommend that traditional IQ tests not be the sole method of assessment in non-Western countries.

VOLUME 20, ISSUE 6

Find and underline four places where the subjunctive is used in the article.

11 Complete the sentences with your own ideas. Use the subjunctive.

1. When you feel depressed, I recommend that _____.

2. If you want to increase your interpersonal intelligence, I suggest

    that _____.

3. If someone has a hard time talking about feelings, it might be important

    that _____.

4. A career counselor might recommend that _____.

12 **WHAT ABOUT YOU?** Read the statements. Do you agree with the opinions expressed? Write your reaction to each statement.

1. "Even if someone scores very high on IQ and EQ tests, it doesn't prove that the person is very intelligent."

    YOU _____

2. "A person is intelligent only if that person has common sense. What good is being able to do math problems in your head if you're unable to function in everyday life?"

    YOU _____

3. "Because high IQs and EQs are crucial to success, schools and businesses should use tests to measure the intelligence of new students and employees."

    YOU _____

> **The Stanford-Binet scale** is the usual standard by which IQs are measured. An average adult IQ score on this scale ranges from 85 to 115. Approximately 1 percent of the people in the world have an IQ of 135 or higher (a score indicating genius or near genius). According to estimates, which of course are an inexact science, Leonardo da Vinci had a staggering IQ of 220!

13 How easy or hard is it for you to focus on a single task for a long period of time? What makes it hard for you to focus? What helps you focus?

_____

_____

_____

_____

14 Read the article.

GET IN THE ZONE

When athletes are so focused on a task that they are unaware of any physical or mental distractions, they are said to be "in the zone." Athletes know that preparing their bodies for competition is only part of a winning formula; mental preparation is just as important. Getting in the zone means getting into your most productive state.

Corporate competition is similar in many ways to athletic competition. Performing well when the pressure's on is as important for business professionals as it is for athletes. In both fields, success depends on performing better than the competition. Focus and mental preparation are the keys to achievement.

MASTERING THESE EIGHT CONCENTRATION SKILLS WILL ENABLE YOU TO GET IN THE ZONE.

• **Planning:** Although it's important to define long-term goals, there are a lot of steps you need to take in order to make these goals happen. The planning skill involves identifying and updating as necessary the smaller steps you need to take in order to accomplish your bigger dreams.

• **Visualization:** Never underestimate the power of the mind. If you can imagine yourself completing a task, then you'll be successful when you're actually doing it, even if the task may be very difficult or new to you. Envision yourself working toward a goal and overcoming obstacles to achieve it.

• **Mental preparation:** Whether it's a big sales pitch or an important presentation, you need to get your mind ready for the task ahead. Some people find it useful to review their notes right before, while others think about something completely unrelated. Find what works best for you and stick with it.

• **Focusing:** For you to produce your best work, every bit of your energy needs to be channeled into the task at hand. You must train yourself to ignore any thoughts or outside stimuli that may distract you.

• **Staying calm:** Anxiety and nervousness can take your concentration away from the task at hand. Techniques such as deep breathing or taking a short break can help you deal with those unpleasant feelings and get back to doing your best.

• **Positive thinking:** Any time you're working on a task, give yourself positive support and feedback. Take time to note what you're doing well and enjoy the feelings of pride that follow. Use positive thinking to instill confidence in yourself and you can be your own biggest supporter.

• **Boosting your energy:** There are times when you'll feel mentally and physically tired as a result of your work. Successful people learn tricks to give themselves that quick pick-me-up needed to get the job done. Next time your eyes start drooping, try eating a high-energy snack such as crackers with peanut butter or taking a brisk walk around the office.

• **Refocusing:** Disappointment and frustration are a part of life and work, so it's inevitable that sometimes you'll experience these emotions. The trick is to recover from these setbacks quickly and redirect your full attention back to what needs to be done.

Now read about the people. For each person, choose one of the eight concentration skills in the article that you think would be most helpful to that person. Explain your answer. There may be more than one correct answer.

1. "I wish I could learn to be a better public speaker. My new job requires me to give a lot of presentations in front of large groups of people. But I'm really shy and when I get up to make my presentation, I panic. Even if I've spent hours rehearsing my speech, I get nervous and forget everything I wanted to say."
   —*Dave Boyle, London, England*

   Staying calm would help Dave relax when he needs to make a
   presentation. I recommend he try deep breathing or taking a break.

2. "I work really well in the mornings, and I usually get a lot done before lunchtime. But every afternoon at about 3:00, I feel like I'm going to fall asleep at my desk! I'm obviously not too productive when I feel like that."
   —*Jennifer Bowers, Wellington, New Zealand*

3. "I was recently given a task at work that I just can't see myself doing. I mean, me, overseeing an entire project? There are so many steps, and it's so involved. I can't imagine how I'm going to get it done!"
   —*Ana Correa de Costa, Brasilia, Brazil*

4. "I work really hard at my job, and to tell the truth, I'm pretty good at it. But I get down on myself sometimes. If things get difficult or stressful, I tend to focus on what I've done wrong or could have done better—and that just kills my self-confidence."
   —*Pietro di Alberto, Milan, Italy*

15 **WHAT ABOUT YOU? Answer the questions.**

1. Describe a time when you reached your achievement zone. How did you feel?

2. Which of the eight concentration skills mentioned in the article in Exercise 14 do you think are the most effective? Which do you think are the least effective? Explain your answer.

3. Think about the last time you had a deadline to complete a project or to take a test. What techniques helped you stay focused under pressure?

16 Read the article about Shakuntala Devi. Then read the statements. Check <u>True</u>, <u>False</u>, or <u>No information</u>, according to the information in the article.

A Mathematical Genius

"It's a myth that numbers are tough," she said. "They are beautiful; one just has to understand them."

Her name was Shakuntala Devi, but she was often known as the "human calculator." Born in Bangladore, India, in 1933, Devi first astounded her uneducated parents with her calculations at just three years of age. By the time she was six, she was showing off her talents by calculating large numbers in front of university students and professors.

Having received no formal training in mathematics, Devi's abilities have stunned mathematicians. Her now-famous mental multiplication of two 13-digit numbers in 28 seconds earned her recognition in the Guinness Book of World Records in 1980. Aside from multiplication and division of very large numbers, she was able to calculate square and cube roots as well as algorithms in her head. She took only 50 seconds to correctly determine the 23rd root of a 201-digit number. (It took a computer over a minute to complete the calculation.) If given any date in the last century, she could identify the day of the week within seconds.

With no formal education—in her own words, "I do not qualify to even get a typist's job"—Devi inspired students around the world to take an interest in mathematics. "It's a myth that numbers are tough," she said. "They are beautiful; one just has to understand them."

Devi's talents were not limited to numbers. As a child, she taught herself to read and write. She described herself as a voracious reader. And having authored 14 books in English, she became a prolific and perceptive writer. Her books range from children's stories to mathematical puzzles to a cookbook for men.

Unlike some geniuses, Devi was witty and outgoing, giving workshops and interviews around the world. Devi died in 2013, at the age of 83.

	True	False	No information
1. Shakuntala Devi had a head for figures.	☐	☐	☐
2. Devi inherited her talents from her parents.	☐	☐	☐
3. To nurture her special talents, Devi received preferential treatment at school.	☐	☐	☐
4. Devi had only average visual and spatial intelligence.	☐	☐	☐
5. Devi showed signs of genius at a very early age.	☐	☐	☐
6. Devi's intellectual genius was determined by years of formal education and training.	☐	☐	☐
7. Devi was gifted with the ability to write poetry.	☐	☐	☐

17 **WHAT ABOUT YOU?** Read the intelligence traits listed in the box. Answer the questions.

curious / inquisitive	perceptive / observant	talented
inventive / imaginative	persistent	witty
open-minded		

1. Which of the intelligence traits do you value in a friend? Explain.

   _____

   _____

2. Which traits do you value in a colleague? Explain.

   _____

   _____

3. Are the traits you value in a friend the same as or different from the traits you value in a colleague? Why?

   _____

   _____

4. Think of someone you believe is very strong in one of the intelligence traits. Give examples to support your opinion.

   _____

   _____

GRAMMAR BOOSTER

A Write two sentences about each person. Use emphatic stress in the second sentence by adding the auxiliary verb <u>do</u> or by underlining the stressed verb <u>be</u>, the modal, or other auxiliary verb.

1. (Derek) not really very observant / has a way with people
   Derek isn't really very observant. He does have a way with people, though.

2. (Amy) isn't good with her hands / has an ear for music

   _____

3. (Gail) doesn't have a knack for learning languages / is talented in other ways

   _____

4. (Kyle) doesn't have much confidence / has all the skills he needs to succeed

   _____

5. (Victor) doesn't have a lot of experience / has a good intuitive sense

   _____

6. (Suri) hasn't found a job yet / is persistent

   _____

7. (Tara) hasn't been to Africa / has traveled to many other countries

   _____

8. (Travis) doesn't have a teaching certificate / would make a great teacher

   _____

B Complete each sentence. Circle the correct word or phrase.

1. If you have time, I suggest **stopping** / **to stop** for lunch at one of those restaurants.

2. The coach recommends **to get** / **getting** a good night's sleep before each game.

3. For the team to be successful, it's essential **to work** / **working** together.

4. Mr. Hammond said it's critical **getting** / **to get** the package to Shanghai by tomorrow morning.

5. It's urgent for you **to start** / **starting** the process today.

6. The airline suggests **to arrive** / **arriving** at the airport check-in counter two hours before an international flight.

C Complete the sentences with the infinitive or gerund forms of the verbs in parentheses.

1. Doctors recommend _____ (exercise) at least three times a week.

2. It's critical that people work _____ (protect) the Earth's environment.

3. I heard that it's necessary _____ (arrive) at the theater two hours before the show starts if you want to get tickets.

4. She advised _____ (seek) help from a local historical society.

5. The teacher suggested _____ (write) an outline to help us organize our ideas.

6. It's important _____ (make) a budget for your personal expenses.

D **WHAT ABOUT YOU?** Complete the sentences in your own way. Use infinitive and gerund phrases.

1. When I was younger, people advised me _____

   _____

2. If a person wants to be healthy, I recommend _____

   _____

3. If a person wants to be successful in life, it's important _____

   _____

"A great victory in my life has been the ability to accept my shortcomings and those of others. I'm a long way from being the human being I'd like to be, but I've decided I'm not so bad after all."
—Audrey Hepburn, actress, model, special ambassador to the United Nations Children's Fund (UNICEF), 1929–1993

A **PREWRITING: BRAINSTORMING IDEAS** Think about your strengths. Choose one and brainstorm ideas. Include ideas on how you got the strength (was it learned or inherited?), its effects on your life, and ways in which you might use it to your advantage in the future.

B **WRITING** On a separate sheet of paper, write about your strength, developing the ideas you came up with through brainstorming in Exercise A. Use the outline below as a guide. Be sure to include connecting words and phrases.

Paragraph 1: State the strength and describe how you think you got that ability.

Paragraph 2: Explain what you have gained as a result of having that strength. Support your ideas with examples.

Paragraph 3: Describe how your strength might help you in the future.

C **SELF-CHECK**

☐ Did my paragraphs follow the outline in Exercise B?

☐ Did I use connecting phrases to focus on causes?

☐ Did I introduce sentences with connecting words or phrases to focus on results?

WRITING MODEL

One of my strengths is my ability to communicate with others. I think I really have a way with people. Because of the fact that my mom is the same way, and I never really had to work at it, I probably inherited the trait.

I think that I have a way with people because they really listen to me. For example, I was class president when I was in high school, and I was able to convince the other student leaders to change their points of view on a few issues. As a result, we made some changes to the school's policies. When I was in college, I had a part-time job at a store in a mall. I learned quickly and was able to teach other workers how to do things. Consequently, I was promoted to manager in less than a year.

My dream job definitely includes working with people. I can't imagine a job where I worked by myself all day. I'm studying right now to become a teacher. I think I'll be a good teacher because I'll be able to use my people skills to connect with students.

What Lies Ahead?

1 Read the advertisements for innovative technologies. Then answer the questions.

Wish you had more time? Add 8 hours to your day!

O. P. Laboratory is currently conducting trials on a new drug that completely eliminates the need for human sleep!

The average person spends one-third of his or her life sleeping. Imagine if you could reclaim all that time by making sleep unnecessary! Just think of all the extra time you'd have available to:

- work extra hours and make more money
- catch up on all those projects around the house
- relax with family and friends
- enjoy hobbies and leisure activities

oplaboratory.com

Under the Sea Development Company

is redefining the idea of "living space."

We're currently developing the world's first underwater city, complete with a school system, a hospital, and a large shopping and entertainment district.

Visit us at underthesea development.com and learn how we're giving people a whole new idea about the place they call home.

Leave the driving to us!

Himoshi Motors is about to change the way you think about driving forever.

Introducing the world's first auto-pilot car! The AutoCar is self-guided and self-driven. You just input the start and destination locations. Then the AutoCar maps out the route and actually drives you, obeying all traffic signals and relying on sensors that "see" and "hear" other vehicles and respond accordingly.

Interested in seeing the prototype for yourself?

Check out **himoshimotors/autocar.com.**

Travel through time with your very own Time Machine!

Just imagine being able to:

- go back in time to change the way you handled a situation
- see how your parents really acted when they were young
- give your kids a firsthand history lesson they'll never forget
- look into the future to see the consequence of your choices and decisions

Call today for your free information kit.
(800) 555-8460

1. Which invention do you think might catch on easily if it were available today? Why?

_____

_____

2. Which invention, if any, do you think might be available before we know it? Why?

_____

_____

3. Which invention do you think would be most beneficial to people? Why?

_____

_____

4. Which invention do you think might open a can of worms? Explain.

_____

_____

5. Which invention might be a case in which the bad outweighs the good? Explain.

_____

_____

LESSON 1

2 **Read the predictions about future technologies. Circle the passive forms.**

a robot used to find bombs

1. According to some scientists, the need for humans to perform dangerous tasks such as firefighting (will be eliminated) in the not-so-distant future. These scientists predict that soon robots are going to be relied on to do jobs that could be unsafe for humans. They hope that before too long dangerous work environments will have been made a thing of the past.

a city of the future

2. In 100 years, cities will have been completely redesigned. They will be much more efficient, and renewable energy sources will have been harnessed so that there is almost no pollution. People will be moved quickly and efficiently from one neighborhood to another by non-polluting air taxis. Very tall skyscrapers will be built, with high-speed elevators to whisk residents up and down quickly. Moving sidewalks are even going to be made available for people who don't want to walk.

3. Within 20 years, the daily commute to work will have been replaced by a short walk from the bedroom to the study. Although face-to-face meetings will still be valued, the majority of people's work will be done in offices in their own home. The need for companies to provide large amounts of office space for employees will be eliminated, and employees won't have to spend time or money to get to their workplace.

an employee at work in a home office

3 **WHAT ABOUT YOU?** Which of the predictions in Exercise 2 is most interesting or exciting to you? Why?

_____

_____

_____

4 Complete the sentences. Use the words in parentheses and the passive voice to express the future, the future as seen from the past, or the future perfect. There may be more than one correct answer.

the Picturephone

1. Because of an increase in automated jobs, fewer people

   _will be needed_____ (need) by manufacturers in the future.

2. In 1970, a telephone that offered both sound and video was developed. Company executives confidently predicted that 3 million of these Picturephone sets _____ (sell) by 1980. However, the Picturephone was a flop.

3. Before the next big outbreak of disease, we hope that emergency plans _____ (make) and precautions _____ (take) by governments.

4. Experts now say that hydrogen fuel cells _____ (accept) as an alternative source of energy within ten to twenty years.

5. By the time the average person can travel into outer space for recreation, many trips _____ (make) to all the planets in our solar system.

6. At the turn of the century, few people ever thought that in twenty years the horse _____ (replace) by the automobile as the primary means of transportation.

7. In 1961, U.S. president John F. Kennedy made the bold promise that a man _____ (send) to the moon before the end of the decade.

5 Rewrite the sentences. Change the underlined part of each sentence from the active to passive voice. Include a <u>by</u> phrase if necessary.

1. Within the next fifty years, <u>scientists will introduce technologies that we can't even imagine now</u>.

   Within the next fifty years, technologies that we can't even imagine now will be introduced.

2. By the year 2050, <u>people will have accepted inventions that seem incredible now</u> as a common part of life.

   _____

3. I thought <u>a secretary would answer the phone</u>, not the boss.

   _____

4. At this time tomorrow, <u>the courier will have delivered the package</u>.

   _____

5. Because of its global themes, <u>audiences all over the world are going to appreciate the film</u>.

   _____

6. After years of war, <u>government leaders will announce news of the peace treaty</u>.

   _____

6 Make predictions in the passive voice about what will or won't be done in the future. Explain your opinions. Use ideas from the box or your own ideas.

achieve world peace	increase food production
control the weather	protect the environment
discover new energy sources	provide education for all children
establish one international language	reduce costs of medication

1. <u>In my opinion, the costs of medication won't be reduced for a long time. Drug companies are making too much money, and they have a lot of power.</u>

2. _____

_____

3. _____

_____

4. _____

_____

5. _____

_____

LESSON 2

7 Put the conversation in the correct order. Write the number on the line.

_____ Because it's a slippery slope. No one knows how this new technology is going to be applied.

_1_ You know, they say that new technologies are going to totally change the way we live our lives.

_____ True. Sometimes technology develops faster than people can decide how it should be used.

_____ Do you really feel that way? How come?

_____ If you ask me, I think that sounds a little frightening.

8 Match each innovative technology with a possible application. Write the letter on the line.

Technology

1. _____ computer chip implants
2. _____ artificial intelligence
3. _____ genetic engineering
4. _____ cloning
5. _____ remote surgery
6. _____ virtual reality
7. _____ nanotechnology

Application

a. Saving endangered species: Genetic material taken from an animal at risk of extinction could be used to create exact copies of the animal.

b. Long-distance health care: A doctor in a hospital in New York could perform an operation on a patient who is in an operating room in Moscow.

c. Increasing food production: The genes of a plant could be manipulated in a laboratory so that it grows to three times its normal size.

d. Surgery from within: microrobots, or tiny robots, will be able to go inside the human body to perform surgery, making many invasive surgeries unnecessary.

e. A car that drives itself: A built-in computer could take complete control of the car, eliminating the need for a human driver.

f. Combat training: Soldiers can improve their aim and combat skills in a wide range of situations, with no danger to themselves or others.

g. Storing medical records: Medical workers could instantly get a patient's complete medical history just by waving an electronic device over his or her arm.

9 **WHAT ABOUT YOU?** Answer the questions.

1. Choose one of the innovative technologies in Exercise 8 or another technology you know about. What are some possible applications for this technology?

Technology: _____

Applications: _____

_____

2. What are some pros and cons to this type of technology?

Pros	Cons

3. What's your final opinion of the technology? Do the potential benefits outweigh the potential problems? Why or why not?

_____

_____

_____

10 Complete the passive unreal conditional sentences. Use the correct forms of the words in parentheses.

1. Can you imagine having a computer chip put inside your body? According to one company that makes computer chip implants, that reality might not be too far away. The company claims that cases of identify fraud ___*might/would be reduced*___ (reduced) if implants ___*were used*___ (use) for identification.

2. At the present time, human cloning is illegal in this country. But some people argue that it should be allowed. They say that if human cloning _____ (permit), information about how certain illnesses develop _____ (learn) from cloning diseased cells.

3. If the severe side effects of the drug _____ (make) public, patients _____ (warned) about them by their doctors. But the company hid the information, causing many people unnecessary pain and suffering.

4. It seems like the possible future applications of innovative technologies are endless. For example, if the technology _____ (develop) further, computer chip implants _____ (use) instead of keys. Imagine waving your computer-chipped hand at your front door to open it instead of inserting a key to unlock it.

5. A number of soldiers were wounded in an attack far from any hospitals. If remote surgery _____ (use) to treat their injuries, many lives _____ (save).

6. Several non-governmental organizations are working to achieve equal rights for all people. The organizations' supporters say that if equal rights _____ (grant) to all people, opportunities for a new way of life _____ (create) for them.

7. In the past, consumers didn't know a lot about the dangers of certain genetically modified foods, so they were popular. If consumers _____ (inform) about the dangers, then the foods _____ (not buy).

11 Complete the passive unreal conditional statements. Use the correct forms of the words in parentheses and your own ideas.

1. If computer chip implants _____ (use) instead of credit cards, _____

   _____

2. If companies _____ (allow) to clone human beings, _____

   _____

3. If the Internet _____ (not / developed), _____

_____

4. If the automobile _____ (introduce) sooner, _____

_____

LESSON 3

12 Complete the sentences with words and phrases from the box. Use correct verb forms where necessary.

absorb / neutralize	native	unregulated
dramatically	turn things around	

1. The Great Lakes, in the northern part of the U.S., used to be quite polluted, but people _____, and now they are much cleaner.

2. Trees and plants _____ carbon, which helps the environment.

3. Development should be planned and supervised by the government. If it is _____, the environment will be harmed.

4. Attitudes regarding our environment have changed _____ in the last decades.

5. Sometimes plants and animals that have come from other parts of the world take over and crowd out the _____ plants and animals.

13 **Read the article.**

Hybrids THE WAVE OF THE FUTURE

Most of us are aware that the cars and trucks that we drive today are powered by a resource that will eventually be used up. Oil, from which we derive gasoline, is a nonrenewable resource, and while experts disagree about how much longer world supplies of it will last, it's inevitable that eventually we'll need to find other ways to power automobiles. Hybrids, or hybrid electric vehicles, provide a practical alternative to traditional gasoline-powered automobiles.

A hybrid electric vehicle (HEV)

The word *hybrid* refers to something that is a mixture of two or more things. Hybrids are automobiles that run on both gasoline and electricity. At low speeds with frequent stops, such as on a city street, the hybrid runs on the more efficient electric motor. To save energy, the engine automatically shuts off when the vehicle comes to a stop, such as at a traffic light, and restarts when the driver puts the car in motion. At the medium or high speeds typical of highway driving, the hybrid operates on its more powerful gasoline engine. The electric motor provides additional power as needed, to help the gasoline engine to increase speed or climb hills. This allows a smaller, more efficient gasoline engine to be used. As a result, hybrids use about half as much gasoline as traditional vehicles.

There are also immediate environmental benefits to driving hybrids. Electricity, unlike gasoline, is a clean energy source that does not release harmful gases into the air. Because hybrids use on average only half as much gasoline as traditional vehicles, they create about half as much pollution. Moreover, the electricity used by hybrids can be generated by renewable resources such as solar and geothermal energy.

If you're still not convinced that hybrids are a good option, then consider the personal advantages to buying this type of vehicle. First of all, hybrids are generally only slightly more expensive than traditional automobiles. With gas prices rising almost daily, imagine the gas in your car lasting you twice as long. You could cut your gas expenses in half. In addition, some governments offer special tax deductions to owners of hybrids or electric vehicles.

Most major carmakers are now producing hybrid options of some of their most popular vehicle models. Based on their growing popularity, it is clear that hybrids are the next big thing in transportation technology.

Choose the best answer to complete each statement.

1. It's important that people reduce their consumption of _____.
   a. geothermal energy
   b. pollution
   c. nonrenewable resources

2. Hybrid vehicles get their power from _____.
   a. waste
   b. solar energy
   c. more than one source

3. Hybrids help protect the environment because _____.
   a. they are powered by nonrenewable resources
   b. they reduce pollution
   c. they are made from recycled materials

4. Vehicles powered by both electricity and gasoline _____.
   a. don't create air pollution
   b. are more efficient
   c. are cheaper to buy than traditional cars

5. Drivers of hybrids have to fill up their gas tanks _____ drivers of traditional vehicles.
   a. more frequently than
   b. twice as often as
   c. half as often as

14 **WHAT ABOUT YOU?** **Answer the questions.**

Would you consider buying a hybrid car? Do you think that they will become popular in your country? Why or why not?

_____

_____

_____

_____

_____

Recycling one aluminum can saves enough energy to power a TV for three hours. There is no limit to the number of times that aluminum can be recycled. The recycling process doesn't compromise the quality of the metal, so it can be recycled again and again.

LESSON 4

15 Look at the graphs. Then read the statements. Check <u>True</u> or <u>False</u>, according to the information.

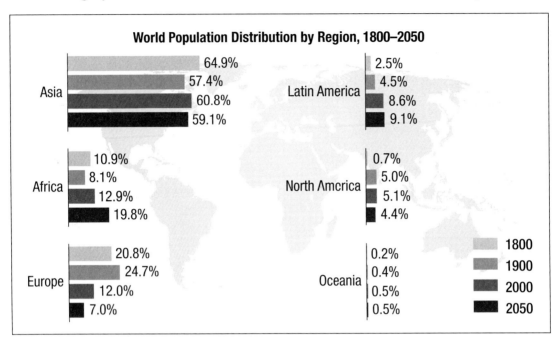

World Population Distribution by Region, 1800–2050

Asia
64.9%
57.4%
60.8%
59.1%

Latin America
2.5%
4.5%
8.6%
9.1%

Africa
10.9%
8.1%
12.9%
19.8%

North America
0.7%
5.0%
5.1%
4.4%

Europe
20.8%
24.7%
12.0%
7.0%

Oceania
0.2%
0.4%
0.5%
0.5%

1800
1900
2000
2050

	True	False
1. The percentage of population increase from 2000 to 2050 is expected to be greater in Africa than the percentage of population increase in Latin America.	☐	☐
2. The largest percentage of the world's population is expected to live in Asia in 2050.	☐	☐
3. Latin America is the only region to show a consistent increase in its percentage of the world's population.	☐	☐
4. North America made the greatest increase in its percentage of the world's population in the last century.	☐	☐

16 Read the article. Then complete each statement, according to the information in the article. Circle the correct word or phrase.

WorldIssues.org

HOME
WHAT'S NEW
POPULATION GROWTH
OTHER GLOBAL ISSUES
RENEWABLE ENERGY
POLLUTION
GENETICALLY-MODIFIED FOOD
MORTALITY RATES
LITERACY RATES
MARRIAGE TRENDS

Population Growth: Four Stages of Development

Population experts studying global population trends have identified four stages that nations experience as they become more developed. In the first stage, both birth and mortality rates are high, so there is little overall growth of the population. Civilization subsisted in this stage for most of human existence, moving into the next stage only within the last 300 years.

In the second stage, improvements in technology and standards of living result in decreasing mortality rates. But the birthrate at this time remains high, so there is a large population growth. Most less-developed Asian and African countries are presently in this stage.

In the third stage, birthrates decrease, resulting in a slower growth rate (if there is any growth at all) in the overall population. This is the case in several European countries, North America, Australia, and Japan, among other places.

A few developed countries, such as Germany and Italy, have now entered the fourth stage of development. In these countries, the fertility rates have dropped so low that mortality rates are actually higher than birthrates, resulting in a decline of overall population.

1. In the first stage of development, birthrates are **low / high** and mortality rates are **low / high**.

2. In the second stage of development, birthrates are **lower than / higher than / the same as** before and mortality rates are **lower / higher / the same**.

3. In the third stage of development, birthrates are **lower than / higher than / the same as** in the second stage. Mortality rates at this time are **lower than / higher than / the same as** in the second stage of development.

4. Canada is in the **first / second / third** stage of development.

5. Birthrates in Germany are **high / low**.

6. A country generally experiences its largest population growth in the **first / second / third / fourth** stage.

> Today it is estimated that 4.3 people are born in the world every second.

GRAMMAR BOOSTER

A Read the following sentences. Write <u>A</u> if the sentence is active or <u>P</u> if it is passive. Circle the passive verbs.

1. _____ Laws to protect the environment must be passed by the legislature.

2. _____ If the company's policy isn't working, then the managers should change it.

3. _____ The president was interviewed by a famous reporter whose articles have been published in magazines around the world.

4. _____ Citizens must show identification in order to vote.

5. _____ The party will be attended by government officials and other dignitaries.

6. _____ After years of failed attempts, the scientist finally discovered the formula.

7. _____ A number of articles have been written on the topic.

8. _____ First sketches of the designs are made, then samples are constructed.

B Complete each sentence. Circle the correct word or phrase in each pair.

1. My hair **had been cut / had cut** right before that picture **took / was taken**.

2. After the apples **pick / are picked**, workers **wash / are washed** them in cold water.

3. Managers **have reduced / have been reduced** prices on everything in the store.

4. A number of possible solutions **will be discussed / will discuss** at the conference.

5. Caution **should be taken / should take** when storing all household cleaners. Parents **must be kept / must keep** all hazardous materials out of children's reach.

6. The winner **will announce / will be announced** later tonight on a special two-hour program.

C Rewrite each sentence in the passive voice. Include a <u>by</u> phrase if necessary.

1. Researchers have conducted numerous studies on the topic.

_____

2. First the chef chops onion, basil, and tomatoes. Then he combines all the ingredients.

_____

3. Patients should take this medication with food to avoid stomach discomfort.

_____

4. The judges declared Patricia Marks the winner of the country's largest singing contest. They awarded her a check for $100,000 and gave her a new car.

_____

5. Passengers must provide tickets and identification before boarding.

_____

6. Members of the health board, who make sure that restaurants meet state health standards, visited The Good Table Café.

_____

A **PREWRITING: PLANNING IDEAS**

You will write an essay about life in the future. Choose a topic and write a thesis statement.

Possible topics about life in the future:

• New technologies

• New uses for existing technologies

• Future population trends

• The environment

• Your own topic: _____

Thesis statement:

On a separate sheet of paper, make an outline to plan the supporting paragraphs of your essay. Write a topic sentence for each paragraph you plan to write. Follow each topic sentence with a list of supporting examples.

B **WRITING** On a separate sheet of paper, write an essay about the topic you chose in Exercise A. Follow your outline. Use your thesis statement and topic sentences. Develop your supporting examples. Don't forget to include an introduction and a conclusion. Refer to the writing model on Student's Book page 108 for an example.

C **SELF-CHECK**

☐ Does my thesis statement clearly state my argument?

☐ Does each of my supporting paragraphs have a topic sentence that supports my point of view?

☐ Does my conclusion summarize my main points and restate my thesis?

UNIT

10

An Interconnected World

PREVIEW

1 Read the people's opinions on language and international communication. Then answer the questions in your own way.

① **Menes Beshay**, Egypt
I don't see why we need to have an 'international' language. That's what translators are for.

② **Callia Xenos**, Greece
I think an international language is a good idea, but I think it should be a created language, like Esperanto, so that no one has the advantage of it being their native tongue.

③ **Alfredo Vivas**, Chile
Sure, it makes sense to have an international language, but why not make it something other than English? I mean, Mandarin Chinese has nearly three times as many native speakers as English. Why don't we learn that instead?

④ **Bianka Gorzowski**, Poland
English is the best choice for an international language because it's already been established as the language of business and science. More websites are in English than in any other language, and it's the most popular second language in the world to learn.

1. Which of the opinions above most closely matches your own?

_____

2. Do you think an international language is a good idea? Why or why not?

_____

_____

3. In your opinion, is English a good choice for an international language? Why or why not?

_____

_____

Esperanto is a created language, constructed in the 1870s–1880s by Dr. Ludovic Lazarus Zamenhof of Poland. Zamenhof wanted to come up with a new language that was relatively easy to learn. He hoped that the language would be used internationally as a tool for communication and that it would help to promote global peace and understanding. Although Esperanto has no official status in any country, there are currently 2 million speakers of the language around the world.

2 Complete each conversation with the correct expression from the box.

a fish out of water	how do you like that	money talks	pulling my leg
a losing battle	it's bad enough that	on the fence	

1. **A:** Have you decided which language you're going to study next?

   B: No, I'm still sitting _____. I can't decide between French and Mandarin.

2. **A:** Where's Bill? The meeting was supposed to start 10 minutes ago.

   B: I don't know. I think _____ he called a 7 A.M. meeting, but now he's not even here.

3. **A:** How are you adjusting to your new job?

   B: Honestly? I feel like _____. But I'll get used to it.

4. **A:** Did you hear that Pete made the Olympic team?

   B: What? Are you _____?

   A: No. It's true.

   B: Well, _____!

5. **A:** Do you limit the time your daughter spends on her phone?

   B: I tried to. But it was _____.

6. **A:** Isn't it awful? ComCorp is going to build a factory on the land that was supposed to become a park.

   B: Really? Well, I guess _____.

3 Complete each paragraph. Circle the correct phrasal verbs to complete the sentences.

1. Based on the following fact, many people say that it's time to **bring about / put up with** changes in global education: It would cost $8 billion to provide basic education to every child in the world. There's no reason why any child should have to **go without / lay off** an education.

2. Scientists say that rising ocean temperatures due to global warming will **carry out / wipe out** plankton, the microscopic plants upon which the ocean's food chains are based. If plans are not **put up with / carried out** to stop global warming, all marine life is at risk of extinction.

3. Cholera is a disease of the large intestine. When a person **comes down with / comes up with** the disease, the results can include rapid dehydration and even death. The current cholera epidemic in Africa has lasted for more than 35 years.

4. In the past few years, factory workers in the U.S. have had to **put up with / bring about** declining wages, higher costs for medical benefits, and longer working hours. Now these workers face a new challenge—companies are **carrying out / laying off** employees and moving their factories to less-developed countries where labor is much cheaper.

4 Complete the chart. Make a list of issues that affect the world today. Identify possible problems that these issues could create, and suggest possible solutions. Then answer the questions.

World issues	Possible negative results	Possible solutions
global warming	rising ocean temperatures wipe out marine life	come up with new energy sources to replace those that cause global warming

1. What global issues are you most concerned about? Why?

_____

_____

2. What global issues are you least concerned about? Why?

_____

_____

5 Read the article. Circle the phrasal verbs.

With restaurants in 119 countries, it's clear that McDonald's has become a global brand. And while there are those who criticize the company's expansion and cultural influence, others explain that individual restaurants, most of which are locally owned, modify their menus to (cater to) local diets and tastes.

a McDonald's restaurant in Riyadh, Saudi Arabia

Check out the menus in McDonald's restaurants around the world, and you'll likely come across a surprising number of unfamiliar choices. For example, you can pick up a McFelafel in Egypt, seaweed burgers in Japan, and rabbit in France. Enter a McDonald's in Italy, and you'll find out that you can order an espresso. Wondering about the McAloo Tikki Burger on the McDonald's menu in India? Try it out—but don't count on it including any beef. In India, you'll have to go without a McDonald's signature hamburger, as the chain's restaurants in that country don't serve beef.

6 **WHAT ABOUT YOU?** What's your opinion of large multinational companies like McDonald's? Do you believe that they add to or take away from local cultures and traditions? Explain your answer.

_____

_____

_____

7 Complete the conversations. Circle the correct phrase in each pair. If both phrases are correct, circle them both.

Conversation 1

Jack: This project isn't coming out the way that I imagined it at all. I think we should

(**1. start it over / start over it**).

Ben: I disagree. People are (**2. counting us on / counting on us**) to finish it before the

deadline. We have a good plan. We just need to (**3. carry it out / carry out it**).

Conversation 2

Amy: Have you been to the new Asian fusion restaurant? I'd love to (**4. try it out / try out it**).

Jason: No, actually I haven't. We could go tonight, but we might have to (**5. put up with a crowd**

/ put up a crowd with).

Amy: Hmm. Maybe we should (**6. put off our visit / put our visit off**). A week night might

be better.

Jason: Good idea.

Conversation 3

Iris: You know, I'm really interested in (**7. taking up knitting / taking knitting up**).

Mary: Really? You should do it. I'm sure you could (**8. pick it up / pick up it**) easily.

Iris: You're right. I'd better start looking for a place that offers classes. Is there any chance I can

          (**9. talk into you / talk you into**) taking them with me?

Mary: Actually, that sounds like fun.

Iris: All right. I'll let you know if I (**10. come anything across / come across anything**).

Mary: Sounds good.

Hooray for . . . Bollywood?

The most popular films in the world do not actually come from Hollywood. Although films from the United States remain very popular worldwide, the Indian filmmaking industry, known as Bollywood, now serves as the primary source of entertainment for more than half of the world's population. While Hollywood releases an average of 475 movies per year, Bollywood is putting out more than three times as many: 1,600 movies per year. According to one BBC poll, the most famous actor in the world isn't an American film star, but Bollywood legend Shah Rukh Khan.

**Indian film star
Shah Rukh Khan**

LESSON 3

8 **Complete the sentences with words from the box.**

exports	homogenization	investments	prosperity
globalization	infrastructure	outsource	

1. _____ has brought many changes, both good and bad, to the world.

2. When governments make more money from _____ that they send overseas, they are

    able to invest more money in the _____ needed to support continued growth.

3. Though globalization has increased _____ and the standard of living in many

    countries, it has also brought many problems.

4. Companies in developed countries _____ many jobs to workers in developing

    countries.

5. Globalization has resulted in a _____ of culture, some critics say, with many

    traditions in developing countries being weakened by closer ties to the rest of the world.

6. Shareholders in global companies expect to make money on their _____ in those

    companies.

9 What changes have you seen in your country due to globalization? Do you see these changes as positive or negative? Why?

_____

_____

_____

10 Read the article.

SWEATSHOPS
The Price of Development?

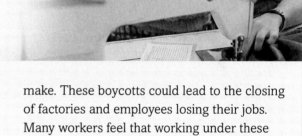

One of the most publicized results of globalization in recent years has been the transfer of well-paid manufacturing jobs from developed countries to less-developed ones, where workers can be paid much less and goods are significantly cheaper to produce.

Critics of this trend have been vocal. In the developed countries where manufacturing jobs are disappearing, labor protesters claim that the resulting rise in the unemployment rate is hurting the national economy. Critics also point out that when the jobs move to developing countries, the working conditions at many facilities in developing countries are far below the accepted standards in developed countries. At these facilities, commonly known as "sweatshops," employees work long hours, often in dangerous conditions, for low pay. Without government laws against child labor, some workers are as young as five years old.

A typical Western response to sweatshops has been to boycott, or refuse to buy, any imports made under these conditions. Surprisingly, however, opinion polls show that most people in developing countries view these sweatshop jobs positively. Although sweatshop workers in developing nations hope for better wages and working conditions, they don't want consumers in developed nations to protest the situation by refusing to buy the products they make. These boycotts could lead to the closing of factories and employees losing their jobs. Many workers feel that working under these conditions is better than having no job at all.

Moreover, some experts point to statistics showing that sweatshop labor has had a positive economic impact on some developing countries. Average incomes for sweatshop workers are now 5 times what they were less than 20 years ago. The working conditions at some factories have improved, as each company tries to attract the best workers. Decreasing infant mortality rates and rising levels of education are indications of an increased standard of living.

While the pros and cons of sweatshop labor continue to be debated, one fact remains clear —the world economy is rapidly changing into one free-flowing global market. The challenge will be to come up with a way to make globalization work for the benefit of everyone.

Now read each statement. Check <u>True</u> or <u>False</u>, according to the information in the article.

		True	False
1.	The article describes workers moving from developing countries to developed countries in search of jobs.	☐	☐
2.	The number of manufacturing jobs in developed countries is rising.	☐	☐
3.	Factories with poor working conditions are known as "sweatshops."	☐	☐
4.	The article presents arguments both for and against sweatshop labor.	☐	☐
5.	Products that are made by low-paid workers are commonly known as "imports."	☐	☐
6.	Some workers in developing countries have decided to stop buying products made in sweatshops.	☐	☐
7.	Statistics show that wages for sweatshop workers in some countries are rising.	☐	☐
8.	Statistics suggest that sweatshop jobs have increased the level of wealth and comfort in some developing countries.	☐	☐
9.	The article recommends that the globalization of the world economy be stopped.	☐	☐

11 **WHAT ABOUT YOU?** Look at the labels of some things you own. List each item and its country of origin below. Then answer the questions.

Item	Country of origin

1. Do you think it's important to buy products that are made in your own country, rather than to buy goods imported from other countries? Explain your answer.

_____

_____

_____

2. Have you ever participated in a product boycott? Do you think that boycotts can be effective in changing bad company practices? Why or why not?

_____

_____

_____

12 **Read one person's experience with culture shock.**

Veronika Soroková

I have been a student here in the United States for three years. It's almost time for me to return to my home country, Slovakia. I'm excited but also a little sad. It took me a while, but I've grown to love living here in New York City. It wasn't always that way, however.

When I first arrived, I was a bit overwhelmed. Some things were the same as at home, but so much was different! All the new stuff was fun for me for a while. I loved trying new food, like New York pizza and sushi. Then there were the stores—such huge stores, with so many items. It was overwhelming trying to figure out what to buy, but all the choices were also fascinating. There were also so many people from different cultures and countries. That was very different from my hometown, where it was unusual to see someone from another country. I loved just people-watching.

But after a few weeks, I began feeling more overwhelmed and less enchanted. Having so many people around me all the time started to get on my nerves. It didn't help that my English needed some work; I couldn't always understand what people were saying. And of course my lack of fluency in English made my classes a little difficult. I was also having a hard time figuring out what kinds of things were okay to talk about and what were not. For example, I learned the hard way that it's not okay to ask someone how much money he or she makes. At home, that wasn't considered rude. And believe it or not, having all those choices when I went shopping started to get annoying, too. I mean, who wants to choose between fifteen different kinds of toothpaste?

I guess I had come down with a case of homesickness. I missed my family, and I missed hanging out with my friends and being able to communicate easily. Speaking of friends, I was having a hard time making any close friends in New York. My difficulty making friends was in part because I hadn't met the right people, and, in addition, I think I was a little withdrawn and depressed.

Finally though, things started to get better. That was in the spring. I had been here for several months, and my English had improved enough that communicating had become much easier. I made a couple of friends in my classes, and that really helped. One friend was from Japan, and one was actually from New York. She took us to all her favorite places in the city, and I discovered some places of my own, including the Conservatory Gardens in Central Park, which were a perfect place to escape the crowds. But you know what? After a while the crowds didn't bother me like they used to. I guess I had just become part of the crowd myself.

Now write the things that Veronika experienced, positively or negatively, for each stage of culture shock.

Stage 1—honeymoon stage

Stage 2—frustration stage

Stage 3—depression stage

Stage 4—acceptance stage

13 **Answer the questions.**

1. What differences between life in New York and life in her hometown were both positive and negative for Veronika?

   _____

   _____

2. What things about your culture do you think might be negative for a newcomer at first but then might become positive with time?

   _____

   _____

   _____

GRAMMAR BOOSTER

A Underline the phrasal verbs in each sentence. Then write **T** if the sentence has a transitive meaning or **I** if it has an intransitive meaning.

1. _____ It's a formal event, so everyone should dress up.

2. _____ After hearing the news, the committee called off the celebration.

3. _____ When I think back on those times, they seem like so long ago.

4. _____ The girl grew up in a small fishing village in the north.

5. _____ It's incredibly rude to cut someone off when they're speaking.

6. _____ Please look your essay over before you send it to your teacher.

7. _____ He agreed to go along with the story, but he wasn't happy about it.

8. _____ Please, sit down and make yourself comfortable.

9. _____ The conference was a little boring, but we came away with some good information.

B Read each sentence. Write <u>T</u> if the sentence has a transitive meaning or <u>I</u> if it has an intransitive meaning. Then match each definition to the way the phrasal verb is used in each sentence.

1. _I_ You're being ridiculous. Stop carrying on like that! — continue

2. _T_ We've carried on many of the traditions from when we were children. — behave in a silly way

suddenly become very angry

3. _____ We blew up balloons to decorate the room for the party.

fill with air

4. _____ A devoted Tigers fan, John blew up when he heard they had lost the game.

end an argument

5. _____ I don't want to fight anymore. Let's make up.

create

6. _____ My grandfather used to make up stories that even the adults loved to hear.

appear

raise, increase

7. _____ Can you turn up the volume on the TV? I can't hear it.

8. _____ After looking everywhere for my keys, they finally turned up under the couch.

C Underline the phrasal verbs in each sentence. Then write <u>A</u> if the sentence is active or <u>P</u> if it is passive.

1. _____ The memo was thrown out because we thought it was trash.

2. _____ Someone used up all the hot water before I could take a shower.

3. _____ The poster had to be done over again because the first one was a disaster.

4. _____ They passed out coupons and prizes at the door.

5. _____ That group of kids always leaves Ginny out when they play games.

6. _____ The passengers on the bus were let off at the corner.

7. _____ The application had been filled out with a blue pen.

A **PREWRITING: GENERATING IDEAS**

You are going to write a rebuttal to an opinion or point of view that you disagree with.

- Choose a controversial issue in your city or country that you're concerned about. For ideas, consider current news topics; governmental laws and policies; or social, cultural, and economic issues.

- First, list the opposing point of view. Then list two or three key aspects of that point of view, with your opposing arguments. If you need more space for your notes, use a separate sheet of paper.

Opposing point of view: _____

Key arguments: _____

_____

_____

My rebuttals: _____

_____

_____

Example:

Opposing point of view: <u>We should not raise taxes on the wealthy</u>

Key argument: <u>If the wealthy pay higher taxes, they will spend less, hurting the economy.</u>

My rebuttal: <u>The increase in taxes will not be enough to change spending habits.</u>

B **WRITING** Many publications include a special section for letters they receive from their readers. Writing a "letter to the editor" is one way to express your opinions on issues that concern you. Choose a newspaper or magazine to write to. Write a letter stating a point of view that you oppose and your rebuttal arguments.

C **SELF-CHECK**

☐ Did I summarize the point of view I want to rebut in my introduction?

☐ Did I rebut each argument by providing details and examples to support my own?

☐ Did I use the expressions and transitions or subordinating conjunctions from Student's Book page 120 to link my ideas clearly?

☐ Did I summarize my point of view in my conclusion?